Idle In The Marketplace At The Eleventh Hour

A new look at the church's most important mandate

David Robinson Ph.D.

ISBN 978-09882588-3-9
ISBN-0988258838

First Edition, September 2012
Printed in the United States of America

Other Books and Leadership materials may be
ordered through booksellers or by contacting:

City Limits International
P.O. Box 6086
Elgin, Illinois, 60121
www.coaching4ministers.co

DEDICATION

I dedicate this book to my wife, Marie. She has been my faithful companion, best friend and ministry partner for nearly five decades. She is the Mother of our three children, David, Lisa and Wendi. She is also the Grandmother of our nine grandchildren, Samantha, Lily, Sarah, Katelyn, Mary, Angie, David, Adam and Stavros, and the Great-grandmother of our great grandson, Rudy. I love them all dearly. They have enriched my life beyond anything I could have ever hoped.

Without her tireless efforts, this book and much of our Kingdom endeavors would never have happened. She has not only influenced my life, but also impacted thousands of children and adults around the world through the God-given gifts and talents of her own.

CONTENTS

FORWARD

"Paul and Silas have caused trouble **all over the world**," they shouted, "and now they are here disturbing our city, too." Acts 17:6

"This same Good News that came to you is going out **all over the world**. It is changing lives everywhere, just as it changes yours that very first day you heard and understood the truth about God's great kindness to sinners." Colossians 1:6 (NLT) All over the world!

In the first reference, Paul is being accused of causing trouble "all over the world" by preaching the Gospel. In the second reference, Paul is giving others the credit for virally getting the Good News out "all over the world." What did Paul know that his accusers did not? That the world will never be reached from the pulpit.

Dave Robinson not only agrees with the Apostle Paul, but he's proven this truth "all over the world" by working tirelessly, in America and overseas, bringing marketplace believers together with ministries to meet people's needs and get the Gospel preached to the whole world.

I know I should call him Dr. David Robinson, but I've known Dave since he was pastor of a Chicago neighborhood church. I was managing a Christian radio station there when he came to me with a program idea called "City Limits." Dave's heart was for the abandoned people of our inner cities. He saw church after church leaving the city limits for the safe, comfortable suburbs, and he realized that the messages filling those voids were not the Gospel of Jesus.

Nothing startling about that.

But what did startle me, after I began sitting under Dave Robinson's ministry, is that he expected ME to get off my butt and minister to these forsaken people!

"Wait! Don't I just drag a few into church, pastor, so you can convert 'em?"

It was then I began to see that this man took the fourth chapter of Ephesians at its word, and he expected us in the seats to do the work of the ministry. However, that wasn't his only...or even his biggest challenge. As Pastor Robinson's influence grew to where he became a pastor of pastors, he found that it wasn't only the "lay people" who had a distorted view of how Jesus expected the Gospel to get out "all over the world." Ministry leaders were also stuck in the "clergy/lay people" mire.

Over the following decades, my professional career evolved into personal finance as a teacher and author, while Dr. Dave's shepherding of pastors and ministry leaders became global. Nevertheless, because we were brothers and good friends, we remained in constant contact.

So I was privileged to see his vision both broaden and sharpen. In the end, however, it is simplicity itself. Jesus used marketplace men and women to build His church...chiefly out in the marketplace. Paul initially tried to build churches through synagogues, but it didn't work. Too much hardening of the attitudes.

So, off to the marketplace he went using marketplace men and women to carry the viral Gospel of Jesus Christ "all over the world."

Dr. Dave could see this marketplace reality from the early days, but it took a lifetime of experiences to distill it down to this book.

This book both convicts and encourages. It charges the "professional ministry" model with its inability to do the Great Commission on its own, while it dares to call marketplace ministers out in the pews equal to those in the pulpit...simply because that's what Ephesians 4 says.

If you're comfortable either on the platform or in the pews, and you don't want anything to rock your "clergy/lay people" boat, drop this book and run. But if you've been thinking that maybe it's time to get the Gospel message "all over the world" using the same strategy Jesus and the Apostles did, this book is a must read!
You'll be learning from one of the wisest and most loving followers of Jesus I have ever known.

John Cummuta, Author
"The Transforming Debt into Wealth© System"

ACKNOWLEDGMENTS

Let me express my deepest gratitude to Mary Jane Kaufman, John Cummuta, Steven Sisler and Geoff Hichborn who gave so much in helping me edit, structure and produce the final draft. They are true friends, prayer partners and some of my greatest supporters. Without them and so many others who marked my life through the years, the book would not be a reality.

John, thank you for the "gentle nudges" that finally worked and I got serious about writing this book and sharing the passion you saw in me with others.

MJ, thank you for your tireless efforts in editing not only this book, but also my monthly e-Leadership Articles for the past several years. Your faithfulness cannot be measured by any standard.

Steven, what can I say? Few have challenged me, as you have to be faithful to my convictions and "get my story out." Thanks for the beautiful job you did on the cover.

Geoff, thank you for allowing God to use the wonderful gift He has given you to bless so many, including me. The service you provided in making this effort a success is appreciated more than you will ever know.

There are so many others that have touched our lives but none more than Tim and Sharon Thomas. We have been best friends since College over 40 years ago. Much of who I am and what God has allowed to happen in our life we owe to their faithful and genuine support in so many areas of life and ministry.

I owe a debt of gratitude to my pastor, Pastor Mark Barclay, for his great example and faithfulness to ministry. To Dr. Raymond Rothwell, who typed so many of my manuscripts, and the wonderful friends he and Mary have been for almost 30 years.

To Pastor Ken Harbaum and the great FGT folks who have been so supportive through the years and all the churches I have been privileged to lead and the wonderful members who loved me in spite of all my failures.

ENDORSEMENTS

I am greatly impressed and blessed with your new book David—it speaks to an extremely important aspect of 'every-day' Christianity that few believers or leaders are aware. I totally endorse your book as one who has lived on both sides of the anointing referenced therein (Ephesians 4:11 & Ephesians 4:1).

In my professional years as a lawyer and my 25 plus years as a pastor, I have seldom found believers or leaders who understand the concepts found in your book! It is essential that believers change the way they view their Christianity and their vocational lives in order to fulfill their life assignments.

Your book "Idle in the Marketplace @ the 11th Hour" is a must-read by Christian leaders/pastors, as well as every Christian working in the marketplace. We must change our thinking, expand our understanding, and begin flowing in the anointing that is rightfully ours, especially the anointing in the marketplace! Thank you David for bringing these truths and revelations to our attention.

Dr. Brian D. Scott
HBA, LLB, D.Min
Victory Christian Centre / Wealth Producers Ministries
London Ontario

....

Idle in the Marketplace is a tremendous book revealing a long lost but severely sought after truth by all pastors and believers. I truly am convicted that every believer everywhere should read this book and ask the Lord Jesus to open his or her eyes to see and receive.

David has been burning in his heart and seeking God for years for this revelation and a way to introduce it to you. He has worked hard to get this book into your hands. I pray that you will read it slowly and meditate on every page. The time has come for all of us to be able ministers of the New Testament! A must read!

Dr. Mark T. Barclay
Pastor, Living Word Church - Midland Michigan
Founder, Righteous Preacher's Network

....

This book carries a message that is much needed in the marketplace today. As I have become acquainted with David Robinson, I have found that he is a man of integrity and extremely gifted with a keen understanding of both ministry and business.

What he presents in his book, *Idle In The Marketplace At The Eleventh Hour*, is a comprehensive and inspiring work of how we as business people can extend our reach to the world in today's marketplace.

Ronny Svenhardt
CEO Svenhardt Swedish Bakery
Exeter California
CEO Business Men's Fellowship
Oakland California

In ministry it is easy to fall into the rut of the urgent, which in turn crowds out issues with eternal value, such as the development of key leaders. Making disciples is leadership development, which just happens to be a very important part of the Great Commission.

I appreciate that David Robinson in his new book, *Idle In The Marketplace At The Eleventh Hour*, has developed this excellent blueprint for recognizing our destiny is the marketplace and not just our daily destination. David gives us a clear vision of what sacred Scripture requires of us and how we can achieve that destiny. He has laid out a bold Biblically accurate course that teaches, inspires and challenges us to become Apostolic leaders in the marketplace, thought leaders, opinion shapers and a body of believers empowered by the Holy Spirit to transform the culture of the nations through principles lived out in the workplace.

Dian Scott
Executive Secretary Business Men's Fellowship
Oakland California

....

I have known Dr. David Robinson for over 40 years. I have watched his growth in God and experienced Dr. Robinson's Godly wisdom first hand. In this book, he well identifies the issues facing the church, ministers, and the business world while taking you through the opposition and problems they face. The world is crying out, even begging for leadership while God's people have abandoned that responsibility to a Godless leadership, especially in the realm of business and politics

"The Church not only needs revival, it needs brains. She desperately needs solid, balanced and Biblical teaching by those called, gifted and anointed for marketplace ministry and the EQ (Emotional Quotient or Emotional Intelligence) necessary for helping people grasp it."

Within these page you will be led from the failure of the church world to victory through a biblical recipe'. Pastors, politicians, ministers, Christian workers, educators, and definitely Businessmen need to read this book.

David R. Griffith
President, Texzon Utilities Ltd
A Christian in the marketplace for over 40 years.

....

It was said of the Apostle Paul that some things he wrote were hard to understand. That is not the case with Dr. David Robinson as he writes with passion and clarity about the Church's failure to respond to Christ's command to make disciples of all nations. While some things he says are very difficult to apply, their truth cannot be denied. He skillfully fleshes out the often quoted, but seldom implemented phrase, every member is a minister and every minister has a ministry! I now have a textbook to go with the quote.

In his well-written and scripturally supported book, Dr. Robinson lays out the Biblical blueprint for fulfilling the Great Commission in our generation. This is not a Pop Christian Culture read, but a passionate appeal to apply these Biblical principles and the change the culture and in doing so; change the character of the world. Read, weep, repent and apply! Thank you Dr. Robinson for your challenging message of hope for our generation.

Dr. Charles Travis
President
Logos University
Jacksonville Florida

....

Idle In The Marketplace At the Eleventh Hour reveals that the number one hindrance to world evangelism is and has been the division that was created between the clergy and the laity, the sacred and the secular, and the full-time and part-time ministries within the Church.

Dr. Robinson reveals that this mindset within the traditional Church is not only unrecognizable in Scripture, but has allowed the enemy to take over and control the governments, educational systems, and the marketplace businesses of the world. This is a non-biblical tradition that Satan has used to infiltrate the Church by forming a ministry class system.

Dr. Robinson reveals that God never intended for a select group to carry the entire responsibility of His program to evangelize and disciple the world. Dr. Robinson takes us on an in-depth look at how the Church can disciple a nation through marketplace ministry.

He identifies the principles and characteristics that are successful in discipling through the sphere of business. His examples give clear instruction and encouragement, so the Church can have a profound influence on the nations, as we follow God's way in fulfilling the Great Commission.

Dr. Dennis Lindsey
President Christ for the Nations
Dallas Texas

....

Dr. David Robinson has not only put together an excellent blueprint, *"Idle In The Marketplace at the eleventh Hour,"* whereby the Churches of America can expand their ministry beyond their four walls, but he has challenged every individual that fills a position in the Market Place to realize that they are a called minister of the Gospel.

The validity of David's ministry is attested in the way he writes with clarity, understanding and compassion. Having known and worked with David for many years, I believe that he has 'lived out' what he has written. God's people, especially pastors/leaders, need to hear, ponder and implement these biblical truths in their lives, churches, organizations and ministries.

Dr. Raymond E. Rothwell
Founder, Leadership Mentoring Ministries
Eaton Ohio

"IDLE IN THE MARKETPLACE" explains the disconnect of the Church from the marketplace that causes a disconnect in effectiveness for building The Kingdom. There really is a "Harvest Field" out there and, as my Pastor likes to say, "We can only get Pastors from the pews, and we can only fill the pews from the street ... so what we are doing to meet people where they actually live?" Dave Robinson's book answers that question powerfully.

Kerry L Fink, CEO
CRMC CRSM TYG Studio Center
Palm Bay Florida

....

This is not just a book. It's a call to action from Dr. David P. Robinson that the church and its leadership must go about doing business differently in order to fulfill its grandest objective—The Great Commission. Robinson's heartbeat revolves around the emergence of apostolic leaders, in accordance with the Ephesians 4 model, that are needed to be the type of salt, with its distinct flavor, in a lost world that Matthew describes in his fifth chapter.

'Idle In The Marketplace At The Eleventh Hour' motivates Christians of all ilk and positions to emulate the visionary work of Jesus outside the four walls of the church as Priority No. 1 by tapping into their spiritual DNA as a royal priesthood. Through a love to evangelize via relationship building while maintaining Christian boldness and integrity,

Robinson details how the marketplace can be turned upside down from its current state of secularism and corruption to being transformed by the power of God if the church acts now through strategic leadership. But time is running short, and the church must take its cue from Jesus' example of passionately affecting the culture where the economy, government and education take center stage.

Dallas Cogle
Southern Maryland Newspapers Sports
Journalist/Church Youth Group Director

....

In this book, my highly experienced ministry coach and friend, David Robinson, demonstrates how the universal plan and calling of God has been hijacked, dividing the Church, and falsely assigning her ministers into disconnected camps never ordained by God. Offering the hope of a rarely experienced but deeply longed for, integrated and motivated *community*; David describes the heart of God to unify these two seriously disparate groups called "clergy" and "laity."

The unification of these groups begins with God's plan for the marketplace in which those who minister according to Ephesians 4:1 are reinforced by and in turn submit to ministers called to an Ephesians 4:11 administration.

David Robinson is an astute observer and compelling witness to the things revealed by the Lord Jesus Christ in our day. Having known David for years, it is no surprise that he has discerned central, yet hidden and eternal truths pertinent to the current and relevant topic of God's gift to the Church of the five-fold ministers and Christians' mandated diligence in the marketplace.

The essence of his work shows that these groups were never intended to work independent of each other.

Given David's extensive experience with pastoral ministry, his work in the marketplace and as a five-fold minister of the Gospel of Jesus, David reveals why the Church has not achieved her full potential and describes in helpful detail the coherent plan God reveals in Ephesians Chapter 4.

Focusing on verses 1 and 11, David shows that the call of God is to neither the clergy nor the laity, but to every believer, in daily life, working in the marketplace as God assigns. David's work drives home the point that whatever our calling and talents, our assignment is to walk successfully in the marketplace as witnesses and encourage those who do, while being in but not part of the world. David shows that this attitude was a central aspect of Paul's life and ministry.

Having begun, run and worked in several for profit and non-profit organizations, I received David's words, full of admonition and instruction, yet also full of promise and hope for both my businesses and for the Church. Marketplace leaders and business people arise: God wants to do great things in your sphere and business, and through them, in the world marketplace as His witnesses.

Geoffey Hichborn, Sr., Civil Engineer
Building Forensics International (Inc.)

Arche' International (501c3, Inc.)
Arche' Africa International, NGO
Anaheim California

....

"Idle in the Marketplace" is a book that needs to be read not only by leadership in the Churches today, but also by every Christian. The message is not just a challenge to believers, what should be a "wake-up call" to everyone.

We often hole up in our churches, and don't forget that every one of us is call to go out into the marketplace to reach the lost! "Idle in the Marketplace" lays out the Biblical principles we need to be following along with guidelines on how to implement these principles.

Dr. Robinson has coached Pastors, churches and businesspersons to be effective leaders in today's world. This book gives each of us the tools to do just that. This book should not be read once, but repeatedly if we want to go change the world for God!

Rev. Steve Biffle
Pastor, Church of the Living Word
Executive Treasurer, "The Fellowship"
President/CEO Biffle & Associates
Columbus Ohio

....

I've had the great privilege of knowing Dr. Dave Robinson for over 30 years. I personally have seen him put this book to work while helping me develop a 140-acre camp and retreat facility known as Fort Courage, in the state of Alabama.

Fort Courage provided ministry for young people First Grade through adults. It was a full service

facility with 22 cabins, 3 homes, Olympic size swimming pool, large recreational area, dining room, 28 horses, and a stagecoach. We had pastors and church leaders to come to utilize the leadership skills that Dave has shared for many years. He was also the Senior Administrator for Canaan Land Bible Training Center. He has helped many men get their life back, and provided the staff with great leadership skills.

I am so happy to see this book come to fruition. This is one of those books you will not want to put down. Believe me, I know.

Mac Gober
President/ Founder of Canaan Land Bible Training Center
Autaugaville, Alabama

NOTES

NOTES

NOTES

INTRODUCTION

The words leaped off the page that morning as I read Matthew 28—*"Make disciples of all nations."* I said, "Lord how do you disciple an entire nation?" As I pondered this, I mused over the idea that the Church has struggled for years making disciples one at time, much less discipling entire nations.

What transpired over the next five to six hours provides the foundation for this book. Fact is, world evangelism and discipleship *must* be the heart and soul of the Church in her efforts to expand the Kingdom of God if it is going to be successful.

The Lord's response was one I did not anticipate when I asked, "How do you disciple a nation?" He said, "Study Exodus, Leviticus, Numbers and Deuteronomy, but from a perspective of discipleship."

As I thought about these four books of Moses, I recalled how Israel came out of Egypt after 430 years of bondage to begin a forty-year journey in the desert wilderness—God's chosen people, oppressed for generations by the Pharaohs at the peak of Egypt's powerful reign were now released. What originally began as a family of 70 Hebrews and no threat to Egypt, had grown to several million over time, an unquestionable threat to the reigning Pharaoh.

Under Moses' leadership they found themselves in the Sinai wilderness loaded down with a formidable amount of Egyptian wealth, but without a government, an educational system, a health system, sanitation guidelines, or other key elements vital to sustaining a new nation—plus they had no definable boundaries in which to call home. They were not a nation with sustainability—they were a mob. However, God would make them one. Over the next forty years, through a process unlike anything they had been previously accustomed too, Israel would undergo the changes necessary to become a force to be reckoned with.

God would disciple them through their forty-year trudge through the wilderness. During these forty years of wandering aimlessly, Israel would make the emblematic mistake of confusing their destiny with their destination. They thought their destiny was reaching the Promised Land—it was not. The Promised Land was only their destination from which their destiny would be fulfilled. According to Exodus 19:6 God said, *"And you will be my kingdom of priests, my holy nation ..."* NLT.

It is in this verse that we understand God's desire for them to do for other nations what He had done for them in the wilderness, but they refused, so God established the priesthood and anointed Aaron and his sons to operate as the only priests serving the people.

This system ended in 1 Samuel 2. Eli, who was the acting priest at that time, failed in his necessary duties as a priest and a father in relationship to both Israel and his sons. His two sons Hophi and Phinehas only made things worse as they increasingly ran amuck about the temple. He rebuked his sons, but the damage had already been done. God had had enough ... he cut off Eli from the priesthood and disallowed any of his family to follow.

God essentially killed the ecclesiastical system and pronounced in I Samuel 2:35:

> *"And I will raise me up a faithful priest that shall do according to that which is in mine heart and in my mind: and I will build him a sure house; and he shall walk before my anointed for ever."* (KJV)

I believe this to be not only a direct reference to Jesus Christ, but also to the Church of our day as well. Moreover, there are traditions in the Church today that we should honor and allow to continue to guide us as they point to significant truths. Traditions are helpful when they remind us of the truths they represent, but more often than not, these traditions become roadblocks to effective world evangelism and discipleship. Unfortunately, modifying or discarding traditions too soon can create even more problems when knee-jerk reactions divide and devour those ill affected by it.

Where is the Church in all of this? They are making the same mistake Israel made—they are confusing their destiny with their destination. Most of us live in line with the premise that our destiny is to go to heaven, but as it was previously with Israel, heaven is our destination from which our destiny will be fulfilled. The destiny of the Church is to rule and reign with Christ forever over His creation—period.

Serving God without the proper destiny creates not only theological and doctrinal debates, but it also promotes a lack of focus and passion for our earthly assignment, which is built upon the continued process of making disciples of all nations. The parallel is clear; not only was Israel originally destined to be a kingdom of priests, but the Church was given this same assignment as well (1 Pet 2:5-9).

"... You are a chosen generation, a royal priesthood, and holy nation, a peculiar people ..." In essence, the Church is called to a kingdom of priests walking in kingly anointing fulfilling kingly duties. In the conversation, John observed in the first chapter of his Revelation, God once again affirms our calling to be a kingdom of priests (1:6). Although the King James Version of scripture uses *"...kings and priests..."* almost every other translation uses a 'kingdom of priests.'

Notice the verb tense in Exodus 19:6 is future. In I Peter 2:5-9 the verb tense is present and in the Revelation, it is past tense (1:6). He was saying to

4

Israel that they should be for him a kingdom of priests. In like manner, to the Church he says we are to be a royal priesthood. We are all called to be priests with a kingly anointing.

If the Church is to have a prophetic impact and effectively address the call for world evangelism and discipleship, she must endorse the mantle of the priesthood for all believers. The purpose of Jesus' death on the cross as well as the infilling of every believer with the Holy Spirit was *not* to set up another *natural* model of dead worship through sacramentally driven trappings, which create little if any activity in the marketplace, but rather a supernaturally charged effort through Spirit led assignments to change this world.

This whole effort we call Christianity today was started by a small business owner named Jesus. He recruited 12 marketplace men when He could have gone to the elite religious training center of his day and chose the top twelve theological students to be on His first world evangelism team. Most of the men He chose would not pass the membership exam of most churches today because according to the book of Acts, they were *unlearned* and *ignorant* men.

They certainly would not be invited to fill a pulpit or join the local ministerial association. According to Paul, they were weak, despised, foolish, and without noble pedigree. Yet Jesus saw something of value in each one and invited them to join his team. Had He chosen men from the school of Gamaliel, the ecclesiastical system of His day, Paul would have joined His team a few years earlier.

Furthermore, it is important to note that God chooses individuals the world would *not* pick if they were assigned the task of looking for a CEO or church leader. Sadly, and more often than not, we in the Church today look for the polished person when looking for leaders. We want to identify only with what we perceive to be successful and accomplished because we believe leaders' to be reflections of us.

After Jesus chose His team, their very short itinerate ministry was underwritten by six entrepreneurial women who believed strongly in Him and His mission—there must be a message in there for the Church today. Has it been ignored, never understood or abandoned in favor of a more polished pastoral model that has not produced apostolic/prophetic impact in the marketplace, government, or institutions of higher learning?

Why is most of the church idle in the marketplace around the world? Why has most of the Church abandoned the Biblical mandate to disciple nations? What will it take to disciple a nation? Do we have Ephesians 4:1 ministers in the marketplace today, or just good Christians minding their own business and working secular jobs? Do Ephesians 4:11 ministers understand their God-given assignment?

Are both groups of ministers in Ephesians 4 taught, trained, equipped, deployed and coached to excellence in their calling to world evangelism and true discipleship? Do both groups see the value of the Divine partnership God intended all along? If so, the church would not be having their lunch handed to them by the humanists, Muslims, Secularists, New Age advocates, and other anti-Christian opponents. Flesh and blood is not our enemy, but evil forces use these belief systems to hinder marketplace evangelism and discipleship throughout the world.

After traveling almost a decade, working full-time with Christian leaders in the church and marketplace, I have found that most cannot defend the faith they claim to believe and are not comfortable sharing their faith when opportunities present themselves. The inability and lack of confidence to share one's faith is one of the leading causes of marketplace idleness today.

The purpose of this book is to address these questions and others, in my passion to see the Church rise with power and authority in every nation and answer the call as citizens, sons, and ambassadors of the Kingdom of Christ.

The Church must discontinue its fight from a position of defensive, but rather she must go to a strategic and planned offence, doing the work by her agenda, not manipulated by the world's game plan. Rather than staying hunkered in the bunker, we must plunge ourselves into the fray, swords wielding.

It is not about how much ground we guard, but how much pilfered ground we raid and take back. Too many of us are sitting around waiting for instructions or the permission to enact that which we already know, but have forgotten.

When was the last time you went into the enemy's camp and took what didn't belong to him? The prophet Amos describes a shepherd rescuing a sheep, "*As a shepherd saves from the lion's mouth only two leg bones or a piece of an ear* ..." (NIV) and image of a frenzied shepherd comes to mind—desperate to retrieve what belongs to him and what was entrusted to his care at any cost.

Too many Christians struggle maintaining personal victory today with little strength left to take on the larger Kingdom issues. Could this be the reason Christian "self-help" books are so popular in the church and the ability to defend and share the "Good News" almost non-existent in the marketplace?

The Church must remain sensitive to the lost, hurting, broken, abused, and abandoned without compromising the Gospel and our call to world evangelism and see nations discipled and fathered. It's time for the Church, gathered on Sundays, to look at how effective they could be when commissioned Monday through Saturday in the marketplace, halls of government, and institutions of higher learning.

Isn't it ironic the text says, *"...idle in the marketplace..."* not idle in the Church?

I contend that if the church is effective in the marketplace, there must be adjustments in Church leaders responsible for the harvesters employed there. The Church is not a Political Action Committee endorsing politicians good or bad. They are not political activists promoting some brand of "liberation theology." Our mission as the Church is not changing the political landscape through endorsements, pressure or activities.

Our mission is being "salt and light" while gathering the harvest in the marketplace. Too much of the Church is trying to change the agenda of un-regenerate people without addressing the reason for it. The moral dilemma that divides the marketplace is a result of the absence of Christ's authority within it. There is no political solution to man's moral problems.

> *"Do you think the work of harvesting will not begin until summer ends four months from now? Look around you! Vast fields are ripening all around us and are ready now for the harvest."* John 4:35 (NLT)

As you will see, there are several themes repeated throughout the book. I believe they are extremely important to generating marketplace activity. Many still say repetition is the best teacher, thus my rationale for including them throughout the book.

1
APOSTOLIC LEADERSHIP PRODUCES MARKETPLACE ACTIVITY

Overcoming idleness in the marketplace requires apostolic-gifted leaders. For too long pastor and teacher gifts have led the church. They are only two of the five Ascension gifts Jesus gave in Ephesians 4. Both are extremely important to the life of any local congregation but ineffective without the other three. Pastors and teachers are necessary to train and support believers already committed to following Christ, but create very little activity in the marketplace.

Local congregations and ministries, led by apostolic leaders, constantly focus on marketplace opportunities that abound any direction you look. Apostolic leaders are energized by what could be and de-energized by what is. They constantly look for creative ways to infiltrate their culture with the Gospel message. Immature apostles, prophets and evangelists tend to be in your face and pushy. However, as those gifts mature through experience and solid teaching, they find ways to affect people's lives without being pushy.

What is an apostolic leader? Someone gifted by God with the ability to create a compelling vision for their marketplace assignment, a plan to carry it out and the ability to build a team to execute the strategy under the leadership of the Holy Spirit.

Apostolic gifted teams, whether they come from a church, organization or business, are mission motivated, energized by today's opportunities, tomorrow's possibilities and de-energized by current management details and responsibilities.

There is a leadership crisis in our world today—not a management crisis. Numerous challenges face leaders in the marketplace, government, and education, and the Church is not exempt. Churches, organizations and businesses are trying to manage their way to a better future. Good managers make today better but do little to create a compelling future.

There are leaders who are great problem-solvers. We call them managers in the marketplace and pastors in the Church. They are vital, and today would be chaos without them. Nevertheless, the greatest shortage is leaders who are goal-setters, team builders and gifted visionaries. They spend most of their time looking through the telescope while the managers peer through the microscope. Managing leaders deal with present reality, while strategic leaders stay focused on the future. What a person does today affects the future, intentionally or unintentionally, no action is without consequence.

The leadership landscape is barren everywhere, especially in the three entities controlling every nation. The first entity is the marketplace, which creates the economy and pays for everything. That is why the Church must bring value to the marketplace if we want to see the transfer of wealth from the heathen to the righteous so often spoken about. The second entity is government. Governments that pass laws and regulations controlling the citizens of every nation. If we ever need the righteous to be in power, it is today.

People mourn all over the world because of corrupt and insensitive government officials. The third entity is comprised of our educational institutions, especially universities. It is in these halls of higher education that the philosophies and values of succeeding generation are determined. Marketplace opportunities come to every generation but only once. We must seize the once-in-a-generation opportunity during the lifetime of that opportunity.

Apostolic-gifted Church leaders must lead the way in

developing marketplace activity. Pastorally gifted leaders always focus on what is happening inside the local Church, as they should, but if we allow that gift to dominate, the marketplace remains idle.

The Church has very defined marketplace responsibilities outlined in Matthew 5:13-16:

> *"You are the salt of the earth. But what good is salt if it has lost its flavor? Can you make it useful again? It will be thrown out and trampled underfoot as worthless. You are the light of the world – like a city on a mountain, glowing in the night for all to see. Don't hide your under a basket! Instead, put it on a stand and let it shine for all. In the same way, let your good deeds shine out for all to see, so that everyone will praise your heavenly Father."*
> *(NLT)*

According to Jesus, the Church is to be salt and light—not in Sunday meetings but in the marketplace every day. Marketplace Christians are on display 24/7. Flashlights are for the dark. We are not in the marketplace to shine our lights on all the sinners but to allow the light of Christ to reveal the good things happening in our lives, giving hope to those still lost in the dark.

The root word for salt in this passage means more than just a preservative. It also means "elite ones"—people who set the standard. Christians are not in the marketplace to maintain a standard set by unbelievers or immature believers. They are there to set the biblical standard with a spirit of excellence. We need to be culturally sensitive but not at the cost of being spiritually incorrect. The Church, through its Ephesians 4:1 ministers, is in the marketplace to provide revelation, set the standard and conserve harvesting results.

Most Church leaders are pastoral (managing) leaders, not apostolic (strategic) leaders. Both are important and necessary for success in the marketplace, but they provide different functions. Pastors are, by definition, managers. They are called to solve problems and provide management on a daily basis for local congregations, organizations and businesses. They deal with spiritual and emotional health issues and administration of management details. You want them on the bus but not driving it.

Leadership's Number One Challenge

The number one challenge for senior leaders, regardless of venue, is knowing the difference between managing today and creating tomorrow. One major reason the church is idle in the marketplace is senior Church leaders are bogged down managing what is already created. I am often asked, "How much time should I spend working on our goals for the future?"

I respond, "If you are responsible for the future you

should be working on them every day." The majority of the senior leader's time should be focused on what is happening in the marketplace and how it affects those who spend most of their lives there. Let the "pastors" (shepherds) manage today's challenges; apostolic leaders must stay focused on the future and the plan for getting there. It does not matter if you lead a church, organization or business. If you are ignorant about or idle in the marketplace, you will soon be irrelevant in most of what you do elsewhere.

By far, the greatest leadership challenge is apostolic leadership, defined by leaders gifted and trained to create a compelling vision, build a team of passionate followers and develop a strategy that is simple yet comprehensive. Does that describe you and your team? Have you figured out if you are a problem solver or a goal setter? Forget your title for a moment and get the basics figured out. You and those you lead will both be happier and more fulfilled.

Where do strategic/apostolic leaders originate? First, let me tell you where they do not come from. They do not come out of academia, seminars, workshops or conferences. Teachers, trainers and consultants cannot produce strategic leaders. You can teach principles, write books, hold workshops and hire consultants, but you can only reproduce who you are. Genesis 1:11-12 says, *"Everything reproduces after its own kind."* (My paraphrase).

For too long local Church leaders have been trained in institutions historically and currently dominated by pastors and teachers. Most people with the pastor or teacher gift are dedicated people, but unable to prepare anyone as a strategic leader or to flow in the apostolic gift, the one most needed for senior leadership. Most Church leaders have their hands full with the internal challenges of church life and the lives of their members. They have little energy left for marketplace concerns. They release their people to marketplace battlegrounds and hope that somehow they make it through until they see them in Church the next Sunday.

Most pastors feel great if their people are in Church "every time the doors are open" but don't have a clue how effective their members are in the marketplace where they spend far more time, energy and resources. Until five-fold gift leaders change that internal focus by making sure their members are adequately taught, trained and equipped, the marketplace remains idle.

First Century Church leaders were strategic (future focused) with apostolic and prophetic gifting's. They appointed deacons, elders and pastors to shepherd and "manage" the growing congregations. How did we get so far away from that model? I contend we moved away from that model by allowing managers in the driver's seat and doing all Church leadership training. Perhaps they never recognized the difference.

Someone who knows the destiny (reason we exist) and destinations (arrival points along the way) needs to be driving the bus of every church, ministry or organization. The driver needs to know the action plan or strategy (a good map) and how to read a compass (set of clear values) when the map gets hard to follow. We call these bus drivers apostolic leaders. You cannot afford to have them back in the seats caring for or entertaining the folks. If apostolic leaders are not driving the bus, the bus winds up in the ditch or you experience a very boring ride. If a manager gets in the driver's seat, the bus seldom leaves the parking lot, but they always try making the ride as comfortable as possible.

All Ephesians 4:11 gifts are vital for success and significance. If they were not, Jesus would not have given them to the Church when He ascended back to the Father. That some gifts are misunderstood, challenge the status quo, or make us uncomfortable at times, is no reason to say they are no longer vital and necessary for today's Church.

I believe much of the confusion, disappointment and frustration inside the Church are caused by the lack of sound teaching on the five-fold gift ministry, and how the gifts of the Holy Spirit leverage the Ephesians 4 gifts Christ gave. If the Holy Spirit came to help us understand Christ, it makes sense the gifts of the Holy Spirit were given to leverage the gifts Christ gave.

"Now these are the gifts Christ gave to the Church the apostles, the prophets, the evangelists, and the pastors and teachers. Their responsibility is to equip God's people to do his work and build up the church, the body of Christ. This will continue until we all come to such unity in our faith and knowledge of God's Son that we will be mature in the Lord, measuring up to the full and complete standard.

We will no longer be immature like children. We won't be tossed and blown about by every wind of new teaching. We will not be influenced when people try to trick us with lies so cleaver they sound like the truth. Instead, we will speak the truth in love, growing in every way more and more like Christ, who is head of his body, the church. He makes the whole body fit together perfectly. As each part does its own special work, it helps the other parts grow, so that the whole body is healthy and growing and full of love." Ephesians 4:11-16 (NLT)

When today's "Sunday" Church begins resembling the First Century Church, you will see activity picking up in the marketplace on Monday through Saturday. Hurting people are looking for that kind of Church to join. They don't see this First Century Church salt and light in most Christians in today's marketplace so they have no desire to follow them to Church.

Apostolic/Strategic leaders fix that if you receive their gift. However, these leaders and their gifts are not welcome in most Churches and organizations today because their theology is dispensational, meaning the apostolic and prophetic roles faded after the "early church" was fully established. As a result, they do not teach their marketplace ministers how to operate them in their marketplace ministry. This is one great reason idleness prevails in the marketplace.

Let's not allow our struggles with titles, offices and pecking order stifle the operation of the gifts that Christ gave. If people with those gifts were embraced and allowed to operate as a team, they would solve most of our internal church problems and create a surge of activity in the marketplace.

To Pastor or not to Pastor

In the Church world, we call everyone responsible for senior leadership "Pastor" whether they have the gift to pastor or not. Given our culture, I do not know how we change that, or even if we should. After 45 years of working in the Church world, I have learned a few things.

- Not everyone called pastor is gifted to pastor or be in the senior leadership position.

- Young people coming out of our training institutions may be students of the Word and they should be. However, pastors and teachers who probably don't have an apostolic gift or knowledge and experience to teach them how to provide strategic leadership have taught these students.

- We call these institutions, "Training Centers" but most do very little training because training is not done in a classroom. You do not train anyone in a classroom. You teach in the classroom but you only train on the job through significant training opportunities.

- If you do not have someone on the core leadership team with an apostolic gift, the church, organization or business is not going to grow, have significance or manifest prophetic impact in the marketplace.

- You can call a person "Pastor," but if they do not have an apostolic gift, they should be pastoring under someone who does. This is not about pride but about effectiveness with each one's gift serving the right purpose.

First Century Church leaders understood they were not independent or codependent, but interdependent. They knew how to develop strategic leaders for taking the Gospel to the marketplace. In turn, these strategic leaders knew how to develop and appoint managers (pastors) and lead them and their members into the marketplace to expand the Kingdom. They refused to be bogged down with the cares of this world or the cares of daily congregational life. They were gripped by what I call "The Five Greats."

The first is, "The Great Commandment," found in Matthew 22:35-40:

> *"One of them, an expert in religious law, tried to trap him with question:*
>
> *"Teacher, which is the most important commandment in the Law of Moses?" Jesus replied, "You must love the Lord your God with all your heart, all your soul, and all your mind." This is the first and greatest commandment.*
>
> *A second is equally important. 'Love your neighbor as yourself.' The entire law and all the demands of the prophets are based on these two commandments."*

It's always the "experts" who want to challenge the true Church and its message. The apostles Jesus empowered certainly had their faults but lack of love and passion for their mission and destiny was not among them. Only love caused the Father to send His Son, only love caused Jesus to suffer the shame and pain of the cross and only love caused every original apostle but two to suffer a martyr's death. One took his own life and the other suffered untold agony and assigned to die on an isolated island.

If not gripped by love, we will not serve with passion and boldness in the marketplace. Only Churches and Kingdom citizens gripped by love find ultimate fulfillment in marketplace activity—"the work of the ministry."

Jesus said the Second Commandment is like the first, "Love your neighbor as yourself." Not like you love God, His Word or even the lost and hurting—but like you love yourself. Loving yourself is not the same as self-love. Most Christians have a hard time liking themselves much less loving themselves.

Don't believe it? Next time you are with a group, ask everyone to write down 25 things they dearly love about themselves. Have you ever thought about it personally? How long is your list?

I believe Jesus meant, "Do you love Who I am in you? Do you love who you are in Me? Do you love the life you now live versus the one I took you out of?" If you do, tell someone. Invite them to follow you as you follow Christ. Someone once said, "Evangelism is one beggar telling another beggar where the bread is."

Forget the first Great if you do not commit to the second, the Great Co-Mission found in Mathew

28:18-20:

> *"Jesus came and told his disciples, "I have been given all authority in heaven and on earth. Therefore, go and make disciples of all the nations, baptizing them in the name of the Father and the Son and the Holy Spirit. Teach these new disciples to obey all the commands I have given you. And be sure of this: I am with you always, even unto the end of the age." (NLT)*

Whereas the first Great is based on love, the second is based on obedience. Obedience not motivated by love soon becomes rebellion. Rebellion in the mind soon gets in your spirit, if not dealt with quickly and decisively soon manifests in behavior. That is why Paul in Romans 12 talks about the "renewing of the mind." Behavioral change always begins with a change of mind.

Most of the Church is idle in the marketplace because they have not made up their mind to change it. Leaders constantly try changing marketplace behavior without a mind (way of thinking) change. Most Christians, and, sad to say, most Church leaders, are satisfied with church attendance and service, what I call Church work. If they were not, things would change. Leaders need to be asking, "Why are you standing idle in the marketplace. Don't you know it's the eleventh hour?" Marketplace evangelism and discipleship is the work of the Church.

It is not called the great option, but the Great Co-Mission. Aren't you glad it is not a mission but a co-mission? We are not alone in the marketplace; we are the house of God and temple of the Holy Spirit. All the power of heaven and the Godhead resides in us. Obedience only comes into to play when clear instructions are given. Even if you have read the Bible hundreds of times or the first time, is marketplace ministry an option we choose or command we must follow?

Theologians will debate the verbs in Matthew 28:18-29 but I believe the text assumes you are "going" and several other verbs outline the strategy for when we go.

"Make disciples of all nations..." Everything done when the church is gathered should prepare and support us in our assignment when the church is scattered. If it does not it ought to be eliminated or assigned lesser importance.

"Baptize them..." This is a public declaration of an inward decision to forsake all and follow Christ. We should make it easy for people to connect with message of the Church, without compromising what it takes to be a disciple (faithful following learner) of Jesus Christ. We should immerse them in the Word, not just water.

"Teaching them to obey" all commands in God's Word in every circumstance. Jesus gave 49

commandments in the New Testament pertaining to discipleship. How many do you know, obey and faithfully model in the marketplace? How many do those you disciple know, understand and faithfully live? What value is a Gospel preached to the marketplace but never modeled in the marketplace? Salvation is based on God's grace and unmerited favor, but discipleship means a very different life and lifestyle. Only true disciples make a difference in the marketplace.

All Christians with marketplace assignments show up. Some show up and turn people off. Others allow the Holy Spirit to show through and attract people to the Jesus in them. Teaching people to obey is about submission to God's word. However, the deeper issue is surrender. It is difficult to submit in the outward act of obedience without first surrendering in your heart. Submission is an action while surrender is an attitude. Yielding to the Spirit's leading is a grace seldom seen in the Church these days much less in the marketplace. Only mature disciples know the difference between submission, surrender and yielding and when to use them.

Where are the Apostles and Prophets?

When the gifts of apostle and prophet lead the church instead of pastor and teacher, you will see order and peace in the church and activity in the marketplace. Our text says "All authority" for the mission was given to Christ by the Father and transferred to the

Church on the Day of Pentecost. The Church for decades, if not centuries, utilized the power of Pentecost to enhance corporate services and Church activities, but somehow overlooked it in marketplace activity. A simple review of the book of Acts shows the power gifts operated primarily in the marketplace. Of the 39 "power miracles" recorded in the book of Acts, all but one happened in the marketplace. Church meetings were given to prayer, study of the Word, fellowship and the Lord's Supper. Sounds like Church meetings were preparation for marketplace ministry.

If the Church is given "all authority" it is time to demonstrate it where it really counts, the marketplace—not just one Church service or conference to the next. If Jesus came to town and had to choose between a convention for Christians or a marketplace opportunity, what do you think He would choose and why? Your answer reveals where you and those you lead are living in light of the Great Co-Mission.

The text ends with a promise that should comfort the fearful and strengthen the obedient. *"I am with you always...." Matthew 28:20 (NLT)* This particular promise of Christ's presence is limited to those obedient to the command to go, baptize and teach. I believe there is a special anointing reserved for individuals, churches, organizations and businesses committed to the final marching orders Jesus gave before leaving earth. You can show up in the marketplace but should never attempt any Kingdom business without relying on this promise. You may or may not "feel" his presence when Divine opportunities present themselves, but you certainly will after that first step of faith taken in obedience to His command. I have experienced it hundreds of times ministering in the marketplace. American Express says, "Don't leave home without it." A better and more effective admonition is, never enter the marketplace without a fresh anointing of the Holy Spirit. Cry as King David in Psalms 92:10, *"Lord, anoint me with fresh oil."*

Forget the Great Commandment and the Great Co-Mission if you don't commit to the Great Opportunity found in John 4:35:

> *"Say not ye, 'There are yet four months, and then cometh harvest?' behold, I say unto you, Lift up your eyes, and look on the fields; for they are white already to harvest." (KJV)*

"Say not" means get rid of all excuses for idleness in the marketplace. For over 30 years, I have prayed almost every day "Lord, help me be sensitive to those You are going to put in my life today." We must train our recreated spirit to be sensitive to what is going on around us every day, not just in the natural world but also in the spirit world. Before we can see the harvest brought in, we must believe God is working in the harvest fields before we arrive. We may not win a soul every day, even every week or month.

However, if we go months and years without a personal harvest, something is wrong somewhere. Making a difference in the marketplace for many begins with "say not."

Then the text says, *"Lift your eyes..."* The Church must not only lift its hearts in prayer, they must lift its eyes to the fields. The harvest is ready because the table is set and the banquet with Christ and the heavenly hosts is ready. I believe the only thing preventing Christ's return is preaching the Kingdom Gospel to all nations, gathering the final harvest and making disciples of all nations.

As end-time harvesters, we must move to the proximity of the harvest that accompanies our call and seize every opportunity our sphere of influence presents. While the Great Commandment is based on love and the Great Co-Mission is based on obedience, the Great Opportunity is based on discernment. Effectiveness in the marketplace requires spiritual awareness. Evangelism is not a *"Holy Ghost mugging mission"* where sinners are overwhelmed with our gospel presentation and surrender out of guilt or pressure. It's simply spiritual awareness of fruit that is ripe for harvesting as we are led daily by Divine appointments.

The fourth Great is the Great Disturbance. The upper room crowd did not go to the Upper Room to develop a strategy for world evangelism. They went in obedience to Christ's final instructions to receive power to be witnesses and fulfill His final command, *"...make disciples of all nations."*

> *"Once when he (Jesus) was eating with them (disciples), he commanded them, "Do not leave Jerusalem until the Father sends you the gift he promised, as I told you before. John baptized with water, but in just a few days, you will be baptized with the Holy Spirit.*
>
> *But you will receive power when the Holy Spirit comes upon you and you will be my witnesses telling people about me everywhere—in Jerusalem, throughout Judea, in Samaria and to the ends of the earth.*
>
> *On the day of Pentecost all the believers were meeting together in one place. Suddenly, there was a sound from heaven like the roaring of a mighty windstorm, and it filled the house where they were sitting. Then what looked like flames or tongues of fire appeared and settled on each of them.*
>
> *And everyone present was filled with the Holy Spirit and began speaking in other languages, as the Holy Spirit gave them this ability."* Acts 1:4, 8; 2:1-4 (NLT)

It's about Jesus

Nowhere does the Bible say we are to get unsaved people to the church building. It says we are to tell them about Jesus. For over 100 years, the church has been debating the meaning of this text. Do all believers have the same experience as those gathered that day during the Jewish Feast of Pentecost? Is the initial physical evidence of Pentecost speaking in "other tongues?" Is this experience for today's church? Do you have any power in the marketplace for witnessing if you do not have this experience? The debate goes on. These questions and many more still hang in the air after more than 2,000 years.

I have my own experience strongly supported by scripture. I am comfortable and content with my theology and doctrinal positions. I have no bones to pick with those with opposing views. This book is not an apologetic on the Biblical meaning of the cited texts. It's an appeal to those who claim Christ as Lord, Savior and King to do something about idleness in the marketplace. I believe without apology the Acts 2:4 experience gives every Christian the best chance for effectiveness, if used for its intended purpose.

Explaining the texts is important, but not nearly as important as going to the marketplace with supernatural power and authority. We can argue about the "initial evidence" but I believe there can be no debate about the substantial evidence of His continuing presence and supernatural activity in the marketplace. Those who oppose the Pentecostal's view on the cited text also oppose most of the other power gifts. It is not about who's most right, but about who's most effective.

31

I love the Nike slogan—"Just do it" in the marketplace and leave the debates for the theologians. Only the power of the Holy Spirit gives the Church the competitive edge she needs to win and manifest prophetic impact.

It's about the Marketplace

We can speak with joy and enthusiasm about the moving of the Spirit in the Church house and we should. It is wonderful to sense His presence when two or more gather in His name. However, we must not allow it to start and end there. Sad to say most revivals start and end in the prayer meeting. What began in the Upper Room quickly spilled into the marketplace and the results speak for themselves. What happened that day? The Great Disturbance was not just for the young Church's benefit alone. It was the start of getting the Gospel of the Kingdom, Jesus so often talked about, to the ends of the earth.

Church networks, Christian publications and books, conferences and stadium rallies play a part, but for the most part the marketplace is still idle after they are gone. There is simply no substitute for every believer showing up every day in every marketplace opportunity, spiritually aware his or her mission is being a witness. Five-fold gifted ministers must know their primary calling is preparing their marketplace ministers for those opportunities.

The final Great gripping these first-century apostles

was the Great Day found in 1 Thessalonians 5:15-18:

"And now dear brothers and sisters, we want you to know what will happen to the believers who have died so you will not grieve like people who have no hope. For since, we believe that Jesus died and was raised to life again; we also believe that when Jesus returns, God will bring back with Him the believers who died.

We tell you directly from the Lord: We who are still living when Jesus returns will not meet him ahead of those who have died. For the Lord Himself will come down from heaven with a commanding shout, with the voice of the archangel, and with the trumpet call of God. First, the Christians who have died will rise from their graves. Then, together with them, we who are still alive and remain on the earth will be caught up in the clouds to meet the Lord in the air. Then we will be with the Lord forever. So encourage each other with these words." (NLT)

The Great Day of the Lord should motivate all Christians in fulfilling their marketplace destiny. Many harvesters stand idle in the marketplace debating when the Great Day is going to take place. Millions of dollars is wasted trying to pin down the day when Jesus returns. Why, when Jesus Himself said only the Father knows. Let's not waste our time discussing when Jesus is returning, where heaven is located or even who is going to make the final cut. Our job is not condemning the lost but sharing the hope the Gospel gives. Every marketplace minister should be a hope dealer not a judge or jury. The Bible says those in darkness know they are lost. Does that mean we sugarcoat the message? Absolutely not, let the hope contained in the message do the convicting.

The Bible says repentance comes by Godly sorrow, not by a sinner-terrorizing message. Jesus said, *"Let the tares and wheat grow together. I'll sort it all out when I come."* Matthew 13:29 (NLT) Let's just be ready. We should be ready at any moment, living a lifestyle of readiness. Let us be faithful with our God-given talent and abilities, not only in church work at the building, but also with the work of the Kingdom in the marketplace. Being ready includes being sensitive to the Holy Spirit at any moment for Divine appointments in the harvest field.

Remember, the target is the harvest field, not the pew. The harvest is where the Five Greats were intended to work. The Great Commandment must be motivated by love, the Great Co-Mission by obedience, the Great Opportunity by discernment, the Great Disturbance by passion for Holy-Spirit power, and the Great Day of the Lord by a spirit of hopefulness.

Traditional pastorally led (gift-not title) Churches and ministries focus primarily on who is already in the fold. Caring for existing members absorbs most of their time, energy and resources. They may talk some or even a lot about the need for activity in the marketplace, but little changes. Evangelism and activity in the marketplace has been reduced to encouraging the saints to pray for their neighbors and invite them to Church, if they are really evangelistic. However, little of either activity takes place on a consistent basis.

Apostolically led Churches and ministries on the other hand focus on the harvest as their primary concern. They are mission driven and not program driven. They eliminate any program not about evangelism and discipleship. Leadership development is not a program or event, but a way of life. Teams are built for discipling new converts and returning them to the marketplace as mature spiritual warriors.

Apostolically empowered ministries make things simple by keeping the marketplace harvest at the center of the bull's eye. They send the spiritually broken and hurting to the infirmary for treatment until they are reasonably healthy and whole. They send the emotionally immature to the nursery to grow up. The committed are sent to the training grounds until they are competent in their gifts and callings and qualify as warriors. The warriors are deployed to the battle for the marketplace.

Many talk about the Matthew 28 calling but forget the Matthew 10 calling. Jesus called His team together and gave them authority with clear instructions for their marketplace assignment. What He describes from verse five on in Matthew 10 does not sound like a walk in the park to me. Boldness in the marketplace seldom comes from seminars and workshops, but from prayer closets filled with God's power and presence.

Apostolic leaders embrace the Five Greats as their primary focus and emphasize the priesthood of all believers. Recognizing the correction Jesus requires in Rev 2:6 and 2:15, they provide no distinction between clergy and laity - only between Ephesians 4:1 and 4:11 ministers. Everyone is a Kingdom builder regardless of location and calling.

They resist the long-standing traditional leadership models, an ecclesiastical system that God never intended. This system claims the priesthood is for all believers but it still functions with a liturgical shadow of religion. There are ministries this system still believes, is reserved for a chosen class, who alone can handle them.

A careful study of I Samuel 2 shows God killed the "system" established under Aaron and his sons. After Eli and his sons became a total disgrace, God said it is no longer about bloodlines and linage, but about whom He would choose based on the condition of the heart and faithfulness.

I believe that is why God put John the Baptist in the

wilderness so when he came as the forerunner of Christ, he would not be identified with the religious system of his day. Tradition would dictate he come as a priest since his father Zacharias was a priest. God broke with tradition and sent John as a prophet proclaiming, *"The Kingdom of heaven is at hand...prepare ye the way of the Lord..."* Matthew 3:2-3 (KJV). He did not go to the temple (our modern-day church) with his message, but to the marketplace where the crowds were.

We are all holy

I've heard pastors and five-fold gifted ministers referred to as "holy men." Thank God, for holy men who fill the pulpits around the world. God knows we have had our fill of the others, but they should not be the only "holy men" in the house. What makes a person holy is not an ecclesiastical system but a relationship with a holy God. Access to a holy God is not the privilege of a few, but an opportunity for all. Jesus provided access to a holy God through His atoning sacrifice on the cross. Upon His death, the veil separating the outer court from the holy place was torn away. No longer was the inner court the private domain for a select few.

The purpose holy men in the pulpit is not so they can report a couple times a week about their great experiences in the Holiest of Holies, but to demonstrate the way all believers can be holy men and women of God. Even Moses invited Joshua into the Tent of Meeting (God's manifested presence) in the wilderness. When we quit calling people "lay people" and open to them the treasurers of the holy place and their right through Christ to live there, maybe they will begin to see their destiny fulfilled in the marketplace.

We have the pulpit model made famous by great preachers such as Calvin, Luther, Spurgeon, Wesley, Whitefield and others. They gained influence in the Church world by their ability to exegete the text and expound truth with great authority. Thank God for great preachers and teachers but the real measure of anyone's preaching is, "Does it produce action and results in the marketplace?"

Currently, a very strong traditional model is the private chaplain for local congregations. They provide shepherding services for the members, and people do need to be cared for. The gift of pastor is a great blessing to any congregation, but it should not be the gift to provide strategic leadership. If the Church's mandated target is the marketplace harvest, the pastoral and teaching gifts do little in addressing that challenge.

A recent model, in the last 40 years, is the executive pastor. This person has the title of "pastor" but they do very little shepherding. Their focus is generating and managing resources. They direct the staff, balance the budget, administrate the office and oversee the programs. Management skills come first and marketplace concerns are barely a passing thought.

Apostles are a different breed

If apostolically gifted leaders lead the Church, best, what do they look like? How does God wire them and what leadership DNA did He give them? I offer five fundamental reasons:

First, they are visionaries. They are passionate about the vision God has given them for the work they lead. They do not claim it is *their* vision, but proclaim, it is our vision. They constantly cast, cultivate and create excitement for the vision. Recruiting, training and inspiring others to join in the pursuit of the vision remain high priorities.

Second, they are mission-minded. To them everything is about Kingdom expansion. They constantly remind themselves, leadership at the strategic level is about change: NOT about "more of the same." A maintenance mentality is something foreign and one they would never allow. They understand, standing still, is really moving backwards. We do everything we can imagine to fill the house on Sunday, while losing ground every day in the marketplace.

If you doubt my premise, look around at your local business community, governments and educational institutions. They are no longer the standard-bearers for Christian values. In most cities in America, and countries around the world, they are the loudest voices of opposition and determined to remove Christ and the Christian life-style from the marketplace at any cost.

Third, developing people always comes before programs. Empowering people and sharing the "ministry" strongly motivates them. Under apostolic leaders, real leadership assignments are always increasing for their team members. Moving people along, up or out of the way is a way of life, not a leadership style. They keep themselves and their teams on a constant learning curve. To keep up with them you must do the same.

Fourth, they function as both mentor and coach to everyone around. It is not what they do, but it is whom God made them. Mentors put things in and coaches pull things out. Mentors teach, impart wisdom and a warrior spirit. Coaches train to perform competently and coach from the sidelines during the game. Great apostolic leaders always have a watchman-coach standing back to back with them examining the views they cannot see at the moment.

Fifth, building teams out of the individuals they develop is how they really exhibit their apostolic leadership ability. It remains their priority—not an option or secondary concern. Great leaders understand the difference between energy and synergy. A group working on the same project with great energy is not the same as a team pulling together toward a clearly defined destination or goal. Teams and teamwork did not originate with man, but with God. In Genesis 1:26—*"God said, let us make man in our image, and let them have dominion..."*

The first team was the eternal Godhead who made man to dominate his environment, including the marketplace. If you are going to dominate, you must do so as a team. Apostolic leaders are passionate about teams and teamwork. Churches, organizations and businesses must ban committees and build teams. Webster's Dictionary defines committee as, "A group of people chosen to consider, investigate and report."

This says nothing about action, accountability or results. True apostolic leaders find it very difficult to work with any group fitting that description. If we want activity in the marketplace, we need to consider our goals when discipling new believers. Are we satisfied with good Church members, or do we want marketplace activists? More than what we want is to know and satisfy the plain demand of scripture.

We need go no further than the example Jesus set. He was a small business owner all His adult life. How did he recruit His first world evangelism team? How did He train them? What were His expectations when He turned them loose and went back to His Father?

First, He never called people out of the world to a life of exclusion or seclusion. There was always the intention they would go back to the world from which they came. The major difference was they went back totally changed from the way He found them. We should be in the marketplace but not allow the marketplace be in us. The marketplace will never be changed by a group of cloistered ministers preaching at it or about its failures. It will change by teaching, training and coaching passionate full-time Gospel ministers called as marketplace ambassadors.

His school of ministry did not involve signing a pledge, passing muster by some ordination committee and then living a separated life as a clergyman. He simply said, "Come be with Me." I know the Church, after Pentecost, established some standards and ways of recognizing God's call on a person's life, but the process has become so encumbered with rights and rituals that marketplace activity by the church has ground to a halt.

Jesus taught His team how to balance the Word with cultural relevancy and produce results by the dynamic of the Holy Spirit wherever He sent them. After you attend a Church service, or live life in the marketplace, is there any evidence you have been there? If not, does it really matter what kind or how many credentials you have?

It's About "Those People" Out There

Jesus constantly looked for ways to connect with sinners. He did not keep His team bogged down in temple activities so they had no time or energy to build relationships with unbelievers. Most Church leaders do not trust their disciples around "sinners" for very long. Most disciples are so weak they do not trust themselves around unbelievers. Most Churches and organizations would do well taking an honest look at their program schedule and see how much it supports the mission assigned in Matthew 28. God is at work in the world, not just in the Church.

We need to find out where and how He is operating in the marketplace, and make it our business to join Him in His efforts. Apostolic leaders constantly teach and reinforce a Kingdom mindset. It is called the Gospel of the Kingdom—not the Gospel of the Institution known as the Church. The footprints of apostolic/strategic leadership are found everywhere marketplace activity is thriving. Here are a few of the results you will see:

One, real ministry opportunities, based on gifting's and not titles, are emphasized for everyone and not reserved for a select few. It is time we stop S.O.S. Christians (those who Slip in, Slump down and Slide out every Sunday) from setting the bar for marketplace commitment.

It is time for the Church to activate the R.O.A.D. warriors, (those Retired on Active Duty). Apostolic leaders *do it* while Pastoral leaders pray and counsel, Teachers find a text, Prophets point out needed corrections and Evangelists make folks feel guilty for not doing it. Not everyone, but the majority by far. If this were not the case, the marketplace would be alive with supernatural activity.

Two, leadership will be team-based eliminating solo roles. Significant ministry will be returned to the people in the pews and not be the guarded domain of Ephesians 4:11 leaders.

Three, ministry scorecards are less about church growth (size of the buildings, budgets and attendance) and more about effectiveness of Ephesians 4:1 ministers in the marketplace. Ephesians 4:11, five-fold gifted ministers, talk more about the performance of their marketplace ministers and less about their platform performance.

Ephesians 4:11 ministers have a new appreciation for their call to train and equip their Ephesians 4:1 marketplace ministers and deploy them to their ministries, not their secular jobs. They teach them how to conserve the results through their apostolic leadership.

Fourth, the command to *"disciple all nations"* in Matthew 28 becomes a reality and not a missions' conference slogan or a message title.

You are Here

Before you make significant changes, be brutally honest about your present reality. Take time with your leadership team and define everyone's current reality. Write it out. I have said for years, "Accurate, adequate and shared information coupled with open and honest communication is the only way to make informed decisions."

What dominates the agenda of your Church ministry calendar and resources—the pews or the marketplace? How many of your members are honestly energized by marketplace opportunities? Is your primary goal making better Church members to fill the house or making passionate missionaries to invade the marketplace? Can your core leadership team competently defend their faith and comfortably share their faith? Is that and expectation, and are they held accountable?

The answer may stun you

Apostolic leaders, the only kind of leaders who should be leading any Church, organization or marketplace effort, constantly ask themselves and their team members these clarifying questions. If you do not ask these questions on a regular basis, I can almost guarantee idleness in *your* marketplace.

2
POSSESSING THE GATES IN THE MARKETPLACE

Bob Dylan wrote a song in 1979 entitled, "When You Gonna Wake Up?" A line in that song reads, "We got gangsters in power and lawbreakers making the rules." Some probably feel these words are too strong and possibly even over the top, but I believe it describes accurately many of today's leaders around the world. Many leaders in America would fit that description given their public and private behavior. Two out of the last three Illinois governors are serving extended sentences in Federal prisons.

They share time with judges, congressional representatives, and other high profile Illinois based government officials. Leadership worldwide is suffering from moral aids (character to resist sin is gone) and increased rebellion against everything just and right. Immunity to sin is gone. Leaders are decaying and dying from within. They hide behind *doing what's right for the people* while making decisions based solely on political and personal gain.

Much of the Church, especially in the West, has shifted to a seeker-sensitive, socially acceptable and politically correct gospel message. While many who have rejected the "politically correct" message have a fatalistic mindset and believe evil is here to stay, the result is focusing their attention on the sweet by and by while awaiting the "great rapture escape."

Instead of invading and affecting the culture with a relevant and effective message, they look the other way in hopes that it will all soon go away or that Jesus runs to our rescue by prying us out of Satan's menacing grasp. The Bible has much to say about the mission for whom the Church is responsible—we are not to go simply and blindly along in order to get along, we are to possess the gates of our enemy.

> *"They (Abraham's servant and his men) gave her this blessing as she (Rebekah) parted: "Our sister, may you become the mother of millions! May your decedents be strong and conquer the cities ("gates" in KJV) of their enemies." Genesis 24:60 (NLT)*

> *"And if ye be Christ's, then are ye Abraham's seed, and heirs according to the promise." Galatians 3:29 (KJV)*

Regardless of your eschatology, every generation has a Biblical mandate to confront evil during their time within the marketplace where life is happening.

We dare not limit our message and influence to the Church pews, but we should endeavor to take it to Wall Street, Main Street, Government and every classroom of higher learning. The Apostle Paul, who spent most of his public ministry in the marketplace, said, "I am not ashamed of the Gospel of Jesus Christ, for it is the power of God unto salvation."

Even John the Beloved said in John 1:12 "But as many as received him, to them gave He power to become the sons of God, (even) to them that believe on his name." This gospel not only has the power to cleanse lost people from their sin while empowering people to live victoriously, but it also has the power to possess the places of authority and public influence. Historically, it seems God's people have surrendered their rightful place of authority and influence.

> *"The kings of the earth believed not, neither all the inhabitants of the world that the adversary and the enemy would enter into the gates of Jerusalem." It is because of the sins of her prophets, and the iniquities of her priests, that they have shed the blood of the just in the midst of her." Lamentations 4:12-13 (ASV)*

The only way evil can win is when God's people surrender ground that rightfully belongs to God's

Kingdom. The Bible says, *"The earth is the Lords and the fullness thereof"* Psalm 24:1. Genesis 24:60 and Galatians 3:29 say God's people would possess the gates (influence) of our enemy and God's seed would bless all nations. Presently the Church is losing the battle for the gates of influence, which begs the question; are we able to reverse this trend?

The Power of Tsaddiqium

Proverbs 11:10 says, "When the righteous (*tsaddiqium*) prosper the city rejoices."

Righteousness exalts a nation. The Hebrew word *tsaddiq* and its plural form *tsaddiqium* are collectively used 250 times in the Old Testament. They appear 50 times in Psalms and 66 times in Proverbs. The Lord is emphasizing that we can be righteous and that He adds values and rewards it greatly.

These words mean much more than some abstract idea of justice or virtue. They represent more than just personal holiness or right standing before God. The real weight the root word carries is the idea of how we live our lives in the marketplace, especially before unbelievers. How do we make those everyday decisions that reveal who we really are when the pressure is on and our decisions have significant consequences?

When our family owned a large recreational vehicle dealership, I constantly faced the challenge of making decisions that were good for business and at the same time reflected the righteousness of God who we claimed to serve. After letting our parts manager go for stealing, I received notice of a wrongful termination suit from the EEOC (Equal Economic Opportunity Commission). My choices were to go directly to Federal Court and try to win the case or to appear before an arbitrator in order to settle the matter. Our attorney said it would cost $50-60,000 just to prepare the case, so we chose the latter.

My attorney and I met with our former parts manager and his attorney before an arbitrator for six hours about two weeks before Christmas. We finally settled for a far less amount than was asked for originally. After all was said and done, the arbitrator looked at me and said, "Mr. Robinson, God has no place in your business."

I responded, "I can't keep him out." Somewhat surprised the arbitrator responded, "Why not?" I quickly replied, "Because every morning I get so filled up with His presence that throughout the day He just leaks out." With that, the arbitrator hastily left the room and I was alone with my former parts manager for the first time that day.

My attorney was making her way to the door, but caught my final remarks to our former parts manager. I told him that I was sorry how things worked and that I wanted him and his family to have a good Christmas. I then asked him to find the time to stop by the dealership and pick up his Christmas bonus that was awaiting him.

At the elevator, I caught up to my attorney and she said, "I could have never said what you said to that young man." I responded, "Without Christ in my heart and business I could not have either. I have to check in with "my boss" every day and give an account of my thoughts, words and deeds. I do not want to have to repent for anything.

If I can't live it (*tsaddiq*), I should not be preaching it." When I stand in my pulpit on Sunday, I need to share with the congregation; with God's help, we can make decisions we could not make without Him. We can truly be the *tsaddiqim* in every situation." The winner that day before the arbitrator was not I, but God. He was glorified and the Kingdom forcefully advanced upon previously stolen ground.

The gates of the cities in the Old Testament were places of decision and influence. This was where matters of mercy, judgment and righteousness for the people of Israel were discussed and decided by the elders—at the gates. Gates were like our local town square or center today. Elders were upstanding citizens and they were known for living lives worthy of that position and responsibility. Proverbs 24:7 tells us that fools have no place or right to hold a position at the gate. Furthermore, Amos 5:10 also observes the unrighteous hate "him who reproves in the gate." With every passing day the *tsaddiqim* (righteous) are less welcome in the gates (places of influence) in America and the West.

There was a time when the Judeo-Christian ethic and morality ruled in America, but no longer. Isaiah's prophetic words have come true. "Our courts oppose people who are righteous, and justice is nowhere to be found. Truth falls dead in the streets, and fairness has been outlawed." Isaiah 59:15 (NLT)

For the past 75 years, it has been losing ground and unless the *tsaddiqim* do something quickly, Humanism, America's new State Religion, intends to obliterate it by the end of the Baby-Boomer generation.

The Ecclesia

When the New Testament writers were looking for a Greek word to describe the First Century Church they chose the word ecclesia. Other words were available that mean assembly or gathering but the Holy Spirit chose ecclesia. This was the word in the Septuagint, the Old Testament word translated into Greek, meaning assembly at the public gate. The assembly of the *tsaddiqim* in the Old Testament is now the assembly of the *ecclesia*, the Church in the New Testament—they are synonymous. The Church should not just assemble on Sundays in the Church house, but in the marketplace the rest of the week— at the *public* gate. Liberals, Humanists, New Agers and atheists are in an all-out war to put the influence of the Church back behind the walls of their church buildings with an end goal of stomping her out altogether. Where once Churches dominated town squares and their steeples filled the skylines of every major city, religious rights are under attack from all directions.

In early America, it was the Church and her leaders who held sway and primary influence in the marketplace, government and education. To prove it you have to go no further than the textbooks 100 years ago. That is why the aforementioned group has put millions of dollars in rewriting the history of America. Just two generations ago, the country looked to church leaders when solving matters of common good. Their wisdom was sought and highly esteemed. Now it is barely tolerated and continuously scorned by the masses.

The mission of the Church goes far beyond having better members and services to provide community acts of benevolence. Those are worthy endeavors, but should not be the extent of her mandate and influence. Those are byproducts of the Church's real mission. Her biblical mandate in Matthew 28 is to go into the entire world, including the marketplace, government and education, preach the Gospel of the Kingdom, make disciples in the local church and send them to confront the enemy in the public arena.

The battle for the soul of America, the Western church and the world in general, is not fought in the church house, but in the marketplace. If the Church ceases to take the fight to the marketplace she will certainly loose. First, she will lose her influence and last she will lose her right to exist as a recognized institution of public influence.

I.   What are the gates and places of influence God's people must possess?

The three entities that control every community, city, state and country are the marketplace that includes business, government and education.   The Church must be about the Father's "business" in all three. What is the Father's business in these three entities? To influence the leadership in all three, if not, evil will take its place. The Church cannot afford to be idle at the eleventh hour.

The **First** gate the Church should influence is business. Business in the marketplace creates the economy. It pays for everything in all three entities. Extending the Kingdom, discipling nations, and spreading the Gospel takes massive amounts of resources today, as does any large endeavor.

Every dollar the Church invests in this effort comes from the marketplace. Someone gifted to obtain wealth (Deuteronomy 8:18) produced something of value in order to earn that wealth. Government does not produce wealth and it never will—it only endeavors to control it. Education does not produce wealth and neither does the Church—they teach us what to do with it. They are simply consumers of the wealth created by those in business.

God, not the world stock markets, determine the Church's financial future as His people live their lives in obedience to what He asks them to do with it.

> "Elisha replied, "Listen to this message from the LORD! This is what the LORD says: By this time tomorrow in the markets of Samaria, five quarts of choice flour will cost only one piece of silver, and ten courts of barley grain will cost only one piece of silver." I Kings 7:1 (NLT)

> "When the Son of Man returns, it will be like it was in Noah's day. In those days before the flood, the people were enjoying banquets and parties and weddings right up to the time Noah entered the boat. People did not realize what was going to happen until the flood came and swept them all away. That is the way it will be when the Son of Man "comes." Matthew 24:37-39 (NLT)

The economy will be a rollercoaster at times. Economic centers will continue to shift around the world, based on many different factors, but God promised in Genesis 8:22, "As long as the earth remaineth there will be seed time and harvest." If the Church looks at the clouds of concern, she will cease to sow and gather the harvest. She will be idle in the marketplace at the very hour she needs to be most active.

Government is the second entity the Church needs to influence. This "gate of influence" passes laws and regulations that control the society of every nation.

> *"Appoint judges and officials for yourselves from each of your tribes in all the towns the LORD your GOD is giving you. They must judge the people fairly. You must never twist justice or show partiality. Never accept a bribe, for bribes blind the eyes of the wise and corrupt the decisions of the godly. Let true justice prevail, so you may live and occupy the land the LORD your GOD is giving you."*
> *Deuteronomy 16:18-20 (NLT)*

If governing challenges the best of God's elect, what does it say for the heathen who try to govern without the wisdom and influence of the Holy Spirit? Judges, those with judicial authority and influence are held responsible for fair judgment. Officers, those with political influence must be responsible for justice. Both carry solemn duties. They must judge fairly, never accept bribes and never twist justice or show partiality. Sorry to say, few public officials serving today could pass that litmus test.

> *"Providence has given our people the choice of their rulers, and it is the duty, as well as the privilege and interest of our Christian nation to select and prefer Christians for their rulers"* —
> John Jay, First Chief Justice United States Supreme Court

The Biblical criteria for political leaders should be the same as Church leaders defined in Paul's Pastoral Epistles, I & II Timothy and Titus. "Select from all the people, some capable, honest men who fear God and hate bribes. Appoint them as leaders over thousand, one hundred, fifty and ten" Exodus 18:21 (KJV). Israel was a republic with a representative government. Some will argue that Israel was a Theocracy but she chose an earthly king to be her leader. In its human organization, Israel's criterion for selecting leaders is still the best for any nation even today.

> "It is alleged by men of loose principles, or defective views of the subject, that religion and morality are not necessary or important qualifications for political stations. However, scriptures teach a different doctrine. They direct that rulers should be men who rule in the fear of God, able to teach men, such as fear God, men of truth, hating covetousness.
>
> However, if we had no divine instruction on the subject, our own interest would demand of us a strict observance of the principles of these instructions. And it is the neglect of this rule of conduct in our citizens, that we must ascribe the multiplied frauds, breeches of trust, peculations and embezzlements of public property which astonish even ourselves; which disgrace a republican government, and which tend to reconcile men to monarchs in other countries and even our own." —Noah Webster,

Author of English Dictionary

America is suffering from moral aids and ethical decay at every level. Greed, abortion, homosexuality, and pornography eat at us internally while New Age Humanism, Islam, Communism and Socialism exploit our weaknesses externally.

Our weaknesses energize our enemies while many of our own leaders get rich at the expense of everyone, especially the poor: sadly, this is nothing new. Many high-profile celebrities have become wealthy off the backs of those for whom they claim to be advocates. They attack capitalism and lobby for equality using a distorted brand of socialism. The financial system they attack is the very system that made them wealthy.

Capitalism is not the problem. Capitalism, *without* the morals to guide it, has caused most of the financial challenges in America and the rest of the world, just as males *without* morality have created a fatherless generation. The root of the problem is as old as scripture itself, *"...the love of money is the root of all evil."* I Timothy 6:10

World leaders continue their search for political solutions that will never solve our moral and ethical decline and eventual destruction.

"America is great because she is good, and if America ever ceases to be good, she will cease to be great." —DE Tocqueville, French

political thinker

I firmly believe God has called a Biblical Christian to fill every public and political office of the land. Can we not find 435 congressional representatives; 100 Senators; 9 Supreme Court justices and 1 president in our nation of 311+ million? If not, why did He say to go into the entire world? Is not government part of the world? If God's (the God of Israel) true believers come into agreement, we should be able to elect 545 people to serve our nation in the fear of God. What are the consequences if we do not?

> *"He that justifieth the wicked and he that condemeth the just, even they both are an abomination to the Lord."* Proverbs 17:15 (KJV)

The ***third*** "Gate of influence" calls us to possess the sphere of education, especially at the university level. The educational arena determines the values and philosophies of every succeeding generation. Values are the soil that nurtures the seeds of our vision. Values are non-compromising principles referred to as the *"old landmarks"* in Proverbs 22:28. We should have at least three sets of values:

- Biblical Values—based on God's vision for the Kingdom and Church.
- Family Values—based on God's desire for Fathers, Mothers and Children.
- Personal Values—based on your God-given destiny.

If we are going to contend for the Faith in our universities and colleges, we must return to their founding principles and values. Harvard University's founding mission was "Truth for Christ and the Church." This statement, embedded on Harvard's shield and many buildings around the campus, gives proof to its original purpose. The original mission of Harvard was training Christian leaders.

Founder John Harvard established Harvard University for training Christian ministers to preach the Gospel. Not just pulpit ministers but ministers called to the marketplace as well. However, over the years its original purpose shifted. Today it is one of the leading centers of humanistic ideology and liberalism. Instead of an asset to the Kingdom, it is one of its greatest threats.

How did this tragic loss happen? With each passing generation, strategic leadership lost its way and influence. The "managers" found a way to gain control and strategic leadership was lost. Instead of turning out great leaders with Christian values, with few exceptions Harvard is now one of the largest purveyors of marketplace leaders *without* a Biblical moral compass.

How sad is it when the managers of America's new State Religion, Humanism, now control most of the leading educational institutions in America, founded on the bedrock of Judeo-Christian principles? The only way you can say they were not founded with a

Christian mission is to rewrite American history, which they have done with fervency.

We are in dire need of Spirit-filled leaders who have sound intellectual credentials, a passion to contend for the faith and a desire to do battle on behalf of the educational institutions in America. Gifted, trained, equipped and affirmed Ephesians 4:1 ministers are the only hope for a return to the educational philosophy that made America great. Philosophy is a system of principles covering knowledge and wisdom that determines individual and corporate worldviews. It took several generations to ruin the Christian philosophy that prevailed in America until the 1960s, but I strongly believe one generation of Ephesians 4:1 marketplace ministers can win it back when affirmed and supported by Ephesians 4:11 ministers.

Ephesians 4:11, five-fold ministers, who believe in their gifted marketplace Ephesians 4:1 ministers, should be their biggest cheerleaders. We must pray, but we must do more than pray. We must recognize and publically support those called to be Ephesians 4:1 ministers in a very tough marketplace environment. Just as we support our young people going into the five-fold calling, we must do no less for our young people called to the marketplace, government and education arenas.

II. WHY WE ARE NOT WINNING THE BATTLE FOR THESE GATES

The Church is not winning because corrupt ministers, imposters not from the Lord, and an out-of-control humanistic government have been in bed together for the past 70 years except for a few brief periods. The slide to where we are today began in the 1930s outlined in *Humanist Manifestos I*, written during that time, and now the State Religion of present day America. Read the following taken directly from the American Humanist website February 2012:

> *"The importance of the document is that more than thirty men have come to general agreement on matters of final concern and that these men are undoubtedly representative of a large number who are forging a new philosophy out of the materials of this world."* —Raymond B. Bragg (1933) Secretary, Western Unitarian Conference

> *"The time has come for widespread recognition of the radical changes in religious beliefs throughout the modern world. The time is past for mere revision of traditional attitudes. Science and economic change have disrupted the old beliefs.*

> *"Religions around the world are under the necessity of coming to terms with new conditions created by a vastly increased*

knowledge and experience. In every field of human endeavor, the vital movement is now in the direction of a candid and explicit humanism. In order that religious humanism may be better-understood are, the undersigned, desire to make certain affirmations, which we believe the facts, our contemporary life demonstrate.

"There is great danger of a final, and we believe fatal, identification of the world religion with doctrines and methods which have lost their significance and which are powerless to solve the problem of human living in the Twentieth Century. Religions have always been means for realizing the highest values of life.

"Their end has been accomplished through the interpretation of the total environing situation (theology or world view), the sense of values resulting there from (goal or ideal), and the technique (cult), established for realizing the satisfactory life. A change in any of these factors results in alteration of the outward forms of religion. This fact explains the changefulness of religions through the centuries. However, through all changes, religion itself remains constant in its quest for abiding values, an inseparable feature of human life.

"Today man's larger understanding of the universe, his scientific achievements, and deeper understanding of society, has created a situation, which requires a new statement of the means and purposes of religion. Such a vital, fearless, and frank religion capable of furnishing adequate social goals and personal satisfactions may appear to many people as a complete break with the past.

"While this age does owe a vast debt to the traditional religions, it is nonetheless obvious that any religion that can hope to be a synthesizing and dynamic force today must be shaped for the needs of this age. To establish such a religion is a major necessity of the present. It is a responsibility, which rests upon this generation. We therefore affirm the following:

First: *Religious humanists regard the universe as self-existing and not created.*

Second: *Humanism believes that man is a part of nature and that he has emerged because of a continuous process.*

Third: *Holding an organic view of life, humanists find that the traditional dualism of mind and body must be rejected.*

Fourth: *Humanism recognizes that man's culture and civilization, as clearly depicted by* *anthropology and history, is the product of a gradual development due to his interaction with his natural environment and with his social heritage. The individual born into a particular culture is largely molded by that culture.*

Fifth: *Humanism asserts that the nature of the universe depicted by modern science makes unacceptable any supernatural or cosmic guarantees of human values. Obviously, humanism does not deny the possibility of realities yet undiscovered, but it does not insist that the way to determine the existence and value of any and all realities is by intelligent inquiry and by the assessment of their relations to human needs. Religion must formulate its hopes and plans in the light of the scientific spirit and method.*

Sixth: *We are convinced that the time has passed for theism, deism, modernism, and the several varieties of "new thought."*

Seventh: *Religion consists of those actions, purposes, and experiences, which are humanly significant. Nothing human is alien to the religious. It includes labor, art, science, philosophy, love, friendship, recreation – all is in its degree expressive of intelligently satisfying human living. The distinction between the sacred and the secular can no* *longer be maintained.*

Eighth: *Religious Humanism considers the complete realization of human personality to be the end of man's life and seeks its development and fulfillment in the here and now. This is the humanist's social passion.*

Ninth: *In the place of the old attitudes involved in worship and prayer, the humanist finds his emotions expressed in a heightened sense of personal life and in a cooperative effort to promote social well being.*

Tenth: *It follows that there will be no uniquely religious emotions and attitudes of the kind hitherto associated with belief in the supernatural.*

Eleventh: *Man will learn to face the crises of life in terms of his knowledge of their naturalness and probability. Reasonable and manly attitudes will be fostered by education and supported by custom. We assume that humanism will take the path of social and mental hygiene and discourage sentimental and unreal hopes and wishful thinking.*

Twelfth: *Believing that religion must work increasingly for joy in living, religious humanists aim to foster the creativity in man and to encourage achievements that add to the satisfactions of life.*

Thirteenth: *Religious humanism maintains that all associations and institutions exist for the fulfillment of human life. The intelligent evaluation, transformation, with a view to the enhancement of human life is the purpose and program of humanism. Certainly religious institutions, their ritualistic forms, ecclesiastical methods, and communal activities must be reconstituted as rapidly as experience allows, in order to function effectively in the modern world.*

Fourteenth: *The humanists are firmly convinced that existing acquisitive and profit-motivated society has shown itself to be inadequate and that a radical change in methods, controls, and motives must be instituted. A socialized and cooperative economic order must be established to the end that the equitable distribution of the means of life be possible. The goal of humanism is a free and universal society in which people voluntarily and intelligently cooperate for the common good. Humanists demand a shared life in a shared world.*

Fifteenth and Last: *We assert that humanism will (a) affirm life rather than deny it; (b) seek to elicit the possibilities of life, not flee from them; and (c) endeavor to establish the conditions of a satisfactory life for all, not merely the few. By this positive morale and* *intention, humanism will be guided, and from this perspective and alignment, the techniques and efforts of humanism will flow.*

So stands the theses of religious humanism. Though we consider the religious forms and ideas of our fathers no longer adequate, the gusto for the good life is still the central task for mankind. Man is at last becoming aware that he alone is responsible for the realization of the world of his dreams, that he has within himself the power of its achievements. He must set intelligence and will to the task."

The first signer of this document was a professor of Church History and Theology at Harvard University. Other signers were Professor of Philosophy at Cornell University, General Editor of Scripps Howard Newspapers and 34 leading scholars, educators and marketplace leaders. The Humanist Manifesto II, written in 1974, confirms the original agenda and reinforces how contrary it is to God and His people. America's young people going to our leading universities and have been fed this ungodly philosophy for the past 80 years are now responsible for the ungodly culture sweeping America.

Now do you understand why America is so distorted and distant from what made her great it's first 200 years? Do you see any similarities in this statement and the twisted philosophical thought and reasoning coming out of our halls of higher learning today? Do you see the need and urgency for today's generation to stop the evil, humanistic thought that has invaded the marketplace, government and education? This may be the last generation that can regain any sort of Christian thought and influence before a total collapse of Christian morality and reasonable debate becomes inevitable.

In Lamentations, 4:13 we see the root cause for America's current behavior the "Sins of the prophets" (guardians of the future) and "Iniquities of the priests" (managers of the present). It is always the enemy's strategy to destroy leaders through false teaching, a corrupt judicial system, and greed in the marketplace. Poor theology and bad behavior have collaborated since the Garden of Eden when Satan asked Eve, "Hath God said?" and God asked Cain, "Where is your brother?"

When the Church is both confused in her theology and a partner in unholy behavior, the whole society suffers. When the Church refuses to resist evil in her own house, she no longer can overcome evil in the marketplace. Evil men of every age use the lukewarm Church to cover up their own wickedness. They covet our endorsement without enduring our message of righteousness and holiness. Note Paul's admonition in II Corinthians 11:13-15:

"For such are false prophets, deceitful workers, transforming themselves into apostles of Christ and no longer marvel; for Satan himself is

> *transformed into an angel of light. Therefore it*
> *is no great thing if his ministers also be*
> *transformed as the ministers of righteousness;*
> *whose end shall be according to their works"*
> *(KJV).*

Why are we not winning this battle? Three key points we must understand are as follows:

First: How we lost the influence over the Marketplace, government, and education in the last 100 years. By teaching poor theology and using such statements as, "Come out from among them and be separate." 2 Corinthians 6:17 (KJV) By setting up an ecclesiastical class system and using designations like clergy, laity, full-time, part-time, bi-vocational, secular, sacred and other abominable terms.

By using, biblical misquotes out of context like "Jesus is coming soon, don't worry about changing the culture—just watch and pray." They mean watch what is going on and pray you are not affected by it. Meanwhile, the enemy walked off with the influence in all three entities because the Church completely abandoned its passion to influence at the sidewalk in front of the Church while they were inside attending a watch-night service.

Second: It is God's will the Church regain her influence being the "salt and light" she was meant to be. Nowhere does scripture indicate the Church should be passive, patsies or pushovers. The Apostle

Paul often referred to Christians as being an army in a constant state of war (see Ephesians 6). No, the Church should not be cutting off the high priest's ear but neither should we allow the enemy to invade the marketplace, government or education as if it belongs to him. The Bible says, *"the earth is the Lord's and the fullness thereof,"* Psalm 24. Flesh and blood is not the enemy, but the evil that controls them is, and we should be doing something about it.

Third: Ephesian's 4:11 ministers must believe its God's will to dominate the influence at these three gates. They must have the will to develop their Ephesian's 4:1 ministers into warriors who know how to do spiritual warfare and win the battle for influence where it matters most. Church leadership must be more than shepherding the flock and making good Church members. Ephesian's 4:11 and 4:1 ministers must believe God together for His plan so that "righteousness" dominates in their city through righteous living and influencing people.

Regaining National and World Influence

Regaining influence begins with understanding the Biblical mandate:

"Righteousness exalth a nation but sin is a reproach to any people" Proverbs 14:34 (KJV).

"When the righteous are in authority, the people rejoice, but when wicked people beareth rule, the people mourn" Proverbs 29:2 (KJV).

The four words that describe what it is going to take are courage, confidence, conflict, and sacrifice. Courage to give your life; one day at a time or all at once like some of our brothers and sisters do in restricted nations. When discouraged you must continue maintaining courage in the face of battle fatigue lest you eventually burn out and give up.

Courage is when you are battle weary, worn out and headed for failure, but then it turns around. Lead with courage is when you are fearful and want to go A.W.O.L., but in your absence of *self,* you decide not to.

Confidence means having faith, not in yourself, but in your God that promised to never leave you or forsake you. He never runs ahead or leaves you behind. Having confidence in your leaders who you are over you in the Lord and guard your spiritual welfare. You need to honor and obey those kinds of leaders according to Hebrews 13. Confidence in yourself and the person God made you. Confident in that you can do all things with the strength God gives.

Conflict. The Bible says, *"They that live righteously shall suffer persecution."* Two Timothy 2:12. I enjoy the good times, but I have learned far more during the tough times. We are called to a battleground, not a playground. Many in the Church today are satisfied with telling you how to be a better person, but better to do what and why? An alcoholic beverage commercial some years ago said, "You only go around once in life. Grab all the gusto you can." It is true you only go around once in this life, but everyone will go on forever in eternity after this life. What you do in this life determines how you live in eternity. We need to be better, but not just for our own enjoyment. It troubles me that so many Church leaders miss the part about arming yourself for spiritual warfare. Many are like the Old Testament Tribe of Ephraim, "Armed for war but turned back in the day of battle" Psalm 78:9 (KJV).

Sacrifice. Regaining the influence over the three entities (gates of influence) requires more sacrifice than many are willing to give. Too much of the Church goes along with evil in order to get along with the world. Result, evil rules. Sacrifice must be more than an occasional giving up something you like. Sacrifice must be a way of life. A spirit of sacrifice illustrated in Mark 10:45, *"For even the Son of Man came not to be ministered unto but to minister and gave His life a ransom for many" (KJV).*

> *"Give me 100 preachers who fear nothing but sin and desire nothing but God, and I care not a straw whether they be clergymen or laymen, such alone will shake the gates of hell (gates of influence) and set up the Kingdom of heaven on earth."* —John Wesley

> *"These are the times that try men's souls. The summer soldier and sunshine patriot will, in this crisis, shrink from the service of their*

country: but he that stands now deserves the love and thanks of men and women. Tyranny, like hell, is not easily conquered; yet, we have this consolation with us, that the harder the conflict the more glorious the triumph. What we obtain too cheap, we esteem too lightly. Heaven knows how to put a proper price on its goods; and it would be strange indeed, if celestial an article as freedom should not be highly rated." —Thomas Paine

We must not consider marketplace challenges without talking about the model Jesus exhibited. He came seeking those who were lost and hurting in the marketplace, not the Temple. The Temple tolerated him for a while, but eventually crucified Him. The marketplace celebrated Him and wanted to crown Him King. Jesus declared war on the religious system while feeling very much at home in the marketplace loving the people there.

Jesus was sensitive to people without compromising the message He came to deliver. His message was an offense to the self-righteous, but one of great hope to the hurting and discouraged. As messengers, we may offend, but we should never be offensive or smug. He never took the path of least resistance. Taking the path of least resistance makes both men and rivers crooked. If the Church has influence in the marketplace, she will swim against the current most of the time.

The Church in the Twentieth Century lost the ability to distinguish light from darkness, sugar from salt, and the roar of the battle from the cheers of the crowd. She is no longer able to preserve righteousness in the midst of evil or lead lost people out of darkness. Jesus said the Church is to be the light of the world. Some Christians are like flashlights—only used in emergencies. Some are like strobe lights—on and off. We need to be searchlights looking for the lost in the marketplace—not to expose their sin, but give them hope.

Jesus said in Matthew 16:18, *"I will build my Church and the gates (influence) of hell will not prevail..."* (KJV). As long as men try building a better Church instead of extending Kingdom influence within the model that already exists—the gates (influence) of hell succeeds.

You do not extend the Kingdom *within* the Church; the Church extends the Kingdom by regaining the influence in the three entities controlling every nation; the marketplace, government and education. Psalms 24:7-10 speaks of these gates, places of influence:

> *"Lift up your heads, O ye <u>gates</u>; and be ye lift up, ye everlasting <u>doors</u>; and the King of glory shall come in. Who is this King of glory? The LORD strong and mighty, the LORD mighty in battle. Lift up your heads, O ye gates. Even lift them up, ye everlasting <u>doors</u>; and the King of*

> *glory shall come in. Who is the King of glory?*
> *The LORD of hosts, he is the King of glory."*
> *(KJV)*

"Gates" are places of influence and "doors" are entry points into the marketplace. Presently in America and most of the world, evil dominates the gates of influence and the doors are shut tight preventing entry of the Gospel where it could do the most good.

Only a spirit-empowered and determined Church can change that. Romans 8:19 says, "The whole world awaits the manifestation of the sons of God" (KJV). What are these sons manifested to do? I contend it is to regain the influence in the marketplace, government and education.

The battle for the soul of America and the free world is raging while the call to arms has sounded. Opportunities are abounding—we cannot see our present lack of influence as much a failure as we should see it as a rallying cry.

Sure, it's a setback, but God did not fall off his throne and the Holy Spirit has not left! The ability to influence the marketplace, governments and the systems of education around the entire world, through current technology, is available. How the Church respond to this opportunity will is the only question that remains.

3
THE GREATEST LEADER EVER TOLD

Four plaques have hung in my office for years. They contain the following quotes from four famous leaders:

> *"The quality of a person's life is in direct proportion to their commitment to excellence regardless of their chosen field of endeavor."*

Most professional football fans will be acquainted with the quote of NFL legend Vince Lombardi recognized for his years with the Green Bay Packers, the winners of the first two Super Bowl championships. Vince Lombardi, because of his commitment to excellence, regardless of what he did or didn't do, set the bar for every other coach for the past 60 years. Other famous quotes are:

"In the middle of every difficulty, lies opportunity." —Albert Einstein

"The pessimist sees difficulty in every opportunity; the optimist sees opportunity in every difficulty." —Winston Churchill

"Things may come to those who wait, but only things left by those who hustle." —Abraham Lincoln

Great leaders and the leadership they offer is not an accident or coincidence—it's the result of years in the crucible of life, fastened with perseverance. Whether it is an NFL football coach, a world-renowned scientist, a national leader during WWII or a United States president leading the charge during our nation's bloodiest war, we see the results of great leadership. They may not have been the best or the brightest examples of great leaders, but they certainly affected my life and helped shape my leadership.

Leadership is everyone's business. In my world, I look at everyone from a leadership perspective. Everyone is a leader at least in two ways. First, if you are a Christian, you are either leading people closer to Christ or further away by the life you live in the Church house, but more so in the marketplace. Second, you are either leading people closer to the vision or away from it by your work ethic and daily performance. You may never be the senior leader of an organization, ministry or business; however, every day you influence the team members around you. This begs the question, is your influence positive or negative?

Leadership is not about elections or appointments to a position. It is not about a place on an organizational flow chart or about having rank and privilege, and it's most certainly not about being the boss or overseer. These may give you opportunities to lead, but in and of themselves, they do not guarantee effective leadership.

Even if you are a leader, the above-mentioned attributes will not guarantee success. Leadership is many things, but *great* leadership is about having an attitude of servant-hood and a sense of responsibility for making a positive difference every day wherever God assigns you. The late Dr. Edwin Louis Cole used to say that you are only able to lead to the degree that you are willing to serve—he could not have been more correct. The effects of your leadership are seen every day *after* you walk away and the team is on their own.

Jesus was the greatest leader and developer of people the marketplace has ever seen. Others may have led more people and produced greater budgets, but no one has come close to influencing the world over a greater length of time with the impact Jesus had.

He trained twelve marketplace individuals from a

broad spectrum of life, who went on to influence the world. From BC to AD, no one has had the same impact that Jesus had in regards to people and change. He worked with a very human team, prone to mistakes and failure and yet the Bible says they "turned their world upside down." Acts 17:6 (KJV) He recruited them from under trees, along riverbanks, from the fishing industry, government tax offices, doctor's offices and back alleys. Some were educated, some illiterate, and many were in between the two.

Some had questionable resumes known as troublemakers and some would cut and run when things got tough. However, He taught, trained and coached them in spite of all their weaknesses. Matthew 10:16 says, He sent them out as "sheep among wolves," (NLT) many times with nothing in the bank and to situations that would make the strongest think twice. Why was He able to garner that kind of commitment? They did it for one reason—so they could be with Him again. They loved being with Him whether it was for a day, a week or eternity.

Good leaders have a way of attracting good people and keeping them for a time. However, great leaders have a way of attracting good people, making them great and keeping them for a long time. I know many people who will work for less money, in less than ideal conditions because they have the opportunity to work for a great leader. Poor leaders find it hard to attract anyone of value and their turnover rate is always high.

Jesus' leadership style was strong in three areas that will always separate the great leaders from good or average. First, He modeled personal excellence. He required nothing of others He did not demand first of Himself. He knew who He was and did not apologize or make concessions. He did not look back over His life from the cross and say, "Wow, I must be the Son of God."

In John 10:36, He declared Himself to be the Son of God, but came as the servant in Mark 10:45. He had no problem washing feet because He knew He made the bodies to which they were connected. You will never reach your full potential and operate in a spirit of excellence at that level until you fully understand who God made you to be.

> *"Jesus knowing that the Father had given all things into his hands, and that he was come from God, and went to God; He riseth from supper, and laid aside his garments; and took a towel, and girded himself." John 13:3,4 (KJV)*

He regularly saw Himself succeeding in the mission God sent Him to accomplish. God constantly made declarations of His success. In Isaiah 55:11 He said, "I declare a thing and it is done for me...my word accomplished what I sent it to do" (KJV) And Jesus offered in John 7:24. "I always do what pleases the Father," (KJV) and in John 11:42, "God answers my prayers." (KJV)

Excellent Speech

Until you master personal excellence, you will never master anything else with excellence. Until you master your tongue, excellence will never be a way of life. It may be a goal you strive for, but until excellence is in everything you do, your leadership may be good, but it will never be great. Excellence starts with your speech. The Bible says your words define your future. Excellence is not in your future until through your words and attitude, it becomes part of your present.

Jesus was always speaking powerful, positive and loving words about His Father, Himself and those on His team. That is why He was welcomed at all the parties and attracted people everywhere He went—performing miracles did not hurt either. By the way, isn't that on the resume of twenty-first century Ephesians 4:1-marketplace ministers? According to Mark 16, it should be a frequent occurrence.

Great leaders understand that excellence starts with them and their in confidence in who God made them to be and who He made them *not* to be. A good friend of mine says, "Knowing who you are is great, but knowing who you are not is greater." They also understand you will never build and lead others effectively by tearing yourself down beyond what is true. The second thing that made Jesus a great marketplace leader was that He did everything with distinction. Mark 7:37 says, "He doeth all things well." I believe every piece of furniture He turned out of His wood shop reflected His spirit of excellence. Because He was the epitome of excellence, the gold standard, everything His hands touched was marked with that same spirit. Every action He took was deliberate and done with excellence and confidence.

A Plan of Action

He said in John 6:38 (KJV), "For I came down from heaven not to do mine own will, but the will of Him that sent me." In John 21:25, it says the world could not contain the books of all the things Jesus did in his three-and-a-half years of earthly ministry if they were all written in detail. I have to believe the quality of His actions and the passion He demonstrated in His efforts never diminished regardless of how many times He performed the task.

As with all great leaders, when Jesus arrived, action took place because every great leader has a bias for action. If something does not change or adjust when you show up, chances are, you are managing and not leading. The only reason for strategic leadership is to make changes necessary to move forward and closer to seeing the vision fulfilled.

Jesus had a plan based on His purpose. All great leaders have a plan based on their goals for the future, whether it is today, tomorrow, next week, next year or in five years. My best estimate is only three out of ten senior leaders have a plan with legitimate goals and use it to guide their daily activities. Everyone else wants God's help, but has no plan or strategy to work with. Solomon says, "We make our plans, but God directs our steps." (NLT)

The Holy Spirit came to live in us and part of His assignment was being our guide. However, He did not come to be a laborsaving device, but rather a labor-enhancing partner. We must grasp the idea that the Holy Spirit is alive and well in the marketplace, not just in church revival meetings.

The Holy Spirit wants to work through us to bring value to the marketplace and build a platform from which to launch our Acts 2 ministry. Too many Christians bring less than maximum value in their marketplace efforts then wonder why their "message" is not received with enthusiasm.

Jesus' marketplace efforts were just as much a part of His message as His prophesying in the temple on Sabbath. Did not He say, "If you give a cup of cold water in My name?" Matthew 10:42 (KJV)

Actions without a plan may bring perspiration, but they will bring very little inspiration. So much time, effort and resources are wasted in churches; the marketplace, government, and education because leaders failed to either plan or plan well. I believe it was General Dwight Eisenhower who said during

WWII, "Even the best battle plans go out the window the moment the first shot is fired." But we still gain much from going through the process.

Managers vs. Leaders

Jesus not only had a plan and acted on it; He formed a team and empowered them to act on their own. Yes, His team failed often, many times disappointed Him, and even deserted Him at critical times, but He never gave up on His method to reach the world. Jesus was part of a team and His entire ministry was built on teamwork.

The Bible says in Deuteronomy 32:26,"One can put one-thousand to flight and two can put ten-thousand to flight." (KJV) This is because God's law of synergy always supersedes His law of energy. Two horses pulling together call pull much more than two pulling separately, even if you combine the weight, that each pulls individually.

You can always distinguish leaders from managers. Give a manager-type an assignment and most will try doing it themselves. Give a strategic leader a job and the first thing they do is find a person to train and develop a team around them to accomplish the task. Someone once said, "Whoever forms a team to carry out the best idea wins."

The third thing that made Jesus an outstanding marketplace leader was He developed excellence in His relationships. He developed relational equity in all but His harshest critics. If you will take notice, most of His disappointments came from the church crowd. Jesus was always making emotional deposits in those who touched His life while the world reaped the dividends. Almost everyone who touched His life was in the marketplace. He walked with His Father in obedience; with His disciples in fellowship, but He walked among the lost as their friend. John 3:17 says, He did not come into the world to condemn it, but to set people free from the curse of sin. (KJV)

Excellence in Relationship

When people meet with you and have relationship, do they feel free or in bondage after the engagement? Such feelings may determine how many friends you have and how long you will have them. Three attitudes characterized the way Jesus displayed excellence in His relationships. The first is found in Mark 10:21, "And Jesus beheld the man and looking fully at Him, loved him" (KJV).

In the Greek *"beheld"* means, "To be fully centered, hold or embrace at that moment." Too often, we see people and even look their way (notice), but if you want to develop excellence in relationships, you must behold them. Be fully centered in on them at that moment.

Some people seem to have a God-given gift to make you feel like you are the only one in the room. Great leaders work on this attitude all the time, especially in the marketplace where transparency and genuineness is not a priority. If you want acceptance and promotion in the marketplace, then learn to behold people as Jesus did for the same reasons. A quicker way to the top may be how you view people and not how you use people.

The second attitude that made Jesus stand out in the marketplace was revealed when He gave them a vision larger than themselves and that would outlast their lifetime. He said, "Follow me and I will make you fishers of men." Matthew 4:19 (KJV) Do not be like the masses who allow television, food, and the internet to trap you when you're bored with life without a vision. The Bible says without a vision, "my people perish." Proverbs 29:18 (NLT) Perishing does not always mean dying. Sometimes it means surrendering to life's challenges and getting lost in something to cover the pain and then just withering away.

Finally, Jesus always had an attitude that gave people something to live for. For Christians, nothing is greater to live for than living for others. It is sad attitudes when the only thing you have to live for is yourself. Many years ago when I was serving as a pastor, my family and I visited one of our parishioners.

She was a retired seamstress from Hart, Schaffner and Marx in Chicago. She never married and with no family to support or encourage her, lived in a tiny three-and-a-half room flat on the north side of Chicago. Often she would check herself into a hospital, faking an illness, just so she would have someone to talk with for a few days. Most of the hospitals she frequented knew her on a first name basis. Sadly, some of our own members avoided her, calling her a hypochondriac. The few neighbors surrounding her avoided her, thinking her to be eccentric. As we shared a meal and tried to find things to talk about, we noticed the only pictures she had around the apartment were all of her, alone. She did not even have a friend to have her picture taken.

You think she would be the exception, but after 45 years of ministry in the Church and marketplace, personal isolation is more common than we care to believe. Do you want to build your relational equity accounts with people? Find a way to make people feel good about themselves and offer them a vision of who they are with your help, and who they can be with God's help.

Empowerment

Jesus also empowered people. He empowered the Church as a whole on the Day of Pentecost, but He also constantly empowered individuals as a way of life. He was always affirming and saying yes.

Yes, I will come to your wedding.

Yes, I will come to your house.

Yes, I will heal your mother-in-law or child.

People asked Jesus over 180 questions in the four Gospels. The most frequent was, "What do you want me to do for you?" How can I not only meet your need, but how can I empower you so you can empower others?" Great leaders always look for ways to make life better for those they are leading. With great leaders, it is always, "What can I do for the team," it's never, "What can the team do for me?"

It's wonderful to have people honor and serve you as their leader, but when you begin to expect their honor, things will begin to go sideways. While you are taking that painful look in the mirror, quote Mark 10:45, *"For even the Son of Man came not to be ministered unto but to minister and give his life a ransom for many."*

The essence of the Bible is about a loving God and trying to convince His children that He loves them and wants more than anything else to give them the very best of heaven's treasure. Why is our Heavenly Father that way? So we can tell those struggling with life there is a better way. This way we can enjoy the life Christ gives every day for the rest of our life. This life prepares us for eternity, the ultimate experience—life everlasting.

Jesus was the greatest leader who ever walked in the marketplace of ideas and people. He was the essence of excellence as a person; by not only the actions He took and the way, He made people feel about them, but by His presence. If we are going to have influence in our marketplace assignment, our calling and ministry, there is no better example to follow and model our life.

Jesus was the greatest Leader who ever lived. He lives today in the hearts of those who call upon His name.

4

THE ROLE OF THE MARKETPLACE AMBASSADOR

The Biblical role of all marketplace ministers is found in II Corinthians 5:20-6:2 and is as follows:

> *"We are Christ's ambassadors, and God is using us to speak to you. We urge you, (unbelieving marketplace contacts) as though Christ Himself were here pleading with you, "Be reconciled to God!" For God made Christ, who never sinned, to be the offering for our sin, so that we could be made right with God through Christ."*

> *As God's partners, we beg you not to reject this marvelous message of God's kindness. For God says, "At the right time, I heard you. On the day of salvation, I helped you." Indeed, God is ready*

to help you right now. Today is the day of salvation." (NLT)

The U.S. State Department guidelines define an ambassador as follows:

"A government representative, called, commissioned and sent to serve in a foreign country for the purpose of accurately communicating the position and policies of the United States of America, so that the people, to whom they are sent, will be brought into and kept in good relationship with the United States of America."

As ambassadors for the King of all Kings, we must do no less. We are representing Him and His kingdom in the marketplaces of America, and everywhere He sends us. We are sent to represent the interests of the King and his Kingdom, not our own. This ability to represent the interests of Christ is a challenge to come by as the apostle Paul stated when writing about Timothy to the Philippians'; "I have no one else like him, who takes a genuine interest in your welfare.

For everyone looks out for his own interests, not those of Jesus Christ" Philippians 2:21 (NIV). Paul knew many people, but he only knew one who had his priorities right. When asked us about our worldviews, I suggest answering in this wise, "My personal views are not important, only those of the

King and the Kingdom I represent."

Often the battle of personal opinions pulls us in when we should be expressing ourselves as Christ's ambassadors. Jesus, Apostle Paul and other First-Century Christians were masters at diverting attention from personal views to Kingdom positions.

In this chapter, we will consider the four elements of being a marketplace ambassador:

1. God's Model Ambassador.
2. The Ambassador's Profile.
3. The Ambassador's Responsibilities.
4. The Ambassador's Goal.

I. God's Model Ambassador

We can learn many things from all great leaders, but only Christ and His Word can adequately prepare us to represent Him and His Kingdom in the marketplace. Jesus set the bar for all of us. How He lived, especially His last three and a half years,

defines our role as Christ's Ambassadors to the marketplace. He mastered three things we would be wise to master ourselves in our calling and marketplace assignment.

Mastering Yourself

First, He mastered Himself. You will never master your marketplace challenges and role as an ambassador, until you master yourself. You will never master yourself until you master your tongue.

"We all make many mistakes, but those who control their tongue can also control themselves in every other way. We can make a large horse turn around and go wherever we want by means of a small bit in its mouth. In addition, a tiny rudder makes a huge ship turn wherever the pilot wants it to go, even though the winds are strong.

"So also, the tongue is a small thing, but enormous damage it can do. A tiny spark can set a great forest on fire. In addition, the tongue is a flame of fire. It is full of wickedness that can ruin your whole life. It can turn the entire course of your life into a blazing flame of destruction, for it is set on fire by hell itself." James 3:2-6 (NLT)

Your words always define you, your calling and your role as an ambassador. The course of events in life and ministry did not puzzle Jesus. He was not shocked when they came, took Him and crucified Him. He knew *Who* He was and *why* He was, at least by age twelve, when He astounded the temple elders with His knowledge and wisdom. He was constantly speaking His Father's word about Himself and not His own:

"I declare a thing and it is done for me. My word accomplishes what I send it to do."

Isaiah 55:11

"I always do what pleases the Father." John 7:29.

"God always answers my prayers." John 11:42

Jesus regularly visualized the success of His life and efforts to represent the values and interests of His Father. He always spoke loving, powerful and confident words about Himself and others. With a few exceptions, the only people He strongly rebuked were the religious managers of His day. If you are not at peace with whom God made you, you will struggle with being His ambassador in the marketplace. You must be able to handle His word "as a workman that needeth not be ashamed," II Timothy 2:15 (KJV) making your message believable and your role as ambassador effective. This is why your message as an ambassador must be clear, competent and simple.

Mastering Relationship

Second, Jesus mastered His relationship. He loved the people He came to give His life a ransom. He celebrated who they were and did not despise who they were not. He inspired them to greatness when they could not see it for themselves. However, more than that, the love the Father had for the people motivated Jesus His entire earthly ministry. The Father's love sent Jesus to die and remove the burden of sin from their shoulders.

Jesus mastered His relationships in three specific ways:

Jesus Focused

First, He beheld them. In Mark 10:21 the writer says, *"And Jesus beheld the man and looking at him loved him."* The word "beheld" means, "to be fully centered or to embrace in the moment." It is difficult to look at people and truly love them if first you do not fully center your attention on them at any given moment. How often have you been talking with someone and their full attention is not centered on you, but somewhere else?

How did it make you feel? Jesus never did that and neither should we, if we want to master our relationships. It is not only rude, but it defeats your ability to be a great leader and marketplace ambassador. If you do not give people your full attention, most of the time, you will not have theirs.

We must consistently monitor how we view and use people whom we have given little attention, much less our love. You can give attention without love, but you cannot love without giving full attention. Jesus is our model for this behavior as He was constantly seeing those, even His "A" team overlooked; blind Bartimaeus, Zacchaeus, the little boy and his lunch, and the lady from Canaan, to name a few.

Too many Christians are overly concerned about how they can meet the famous and pass by those who the

Bible calls the "Greatest of all" in His Kingdom. If you learn how to "behold" the least, you will have no problem with meeting and greeting all the greats, near-greats and even a few not so greats, but think they are.

The Larger Image

Second, Jesus gave each person who would listen, a vision larger than they had for themselves. He told the local expert fishermen, "Follow me and I will make you fishers of men," in Matthew 4:19. Jesus had a way of helping people who had no room in their mirror except for themselves. He helped them find room for someone else. You will never master your relationships if all you do is talk about yourself.

Most of the people you meet in the marketplace as Christ's ambassadors have very little room in their mirror of life for anyone but themselves. Bring them into your world and expose the greatness of God in your life, and you earn the right to speak into theirs. Your role, as an ambassador, is diverting attention away from their daily radar screen challenges and helping them view the possibilities God has for them, only seen through the telescope.

Empowering Others for Greatness

Jesus empowered people for greatness. In Mark 10:36, Jesus asked, *"What should I do for you?* Jesus asks that question many times in the New Testament. His ambassadors are about serving, not being served.

Too many "greats" in the Kingdom are playing musical chairs; everyone is trying to find a throne to sit on when the music stops, rather than taking the towel and basin and looking for opportunities to serve. We see this "presto-change-o" within our own government today. Where we once had servants, we now have mercenaries.

Opportunities abound in the marketplace as well as within the church-world for servant-leaders. Why is it when it is time to move the piano, everyone wants to grab the bench? Too many in the Church look for pulpits to preach from like many in the marketplace look for companies to run, instead of both looking for places to serve. Great ambassadors, go first as servants and earn the right to offer opinions. Even Jesus said in Mark 10:45,

> *"For even the Son of Man came, not to be ministered unto but to minister and give His life a ransom for many."* (KJV)

The essence of God's Word is about a loving Father trying to convince His children that He loves them and is eager to give them the best He has. Our role as marketplace ambassadors has this same essence; we are here to serve, not looking to be served.

Mastering Your Actions

Third, Jesus mastered His actions. John 21:24-25 says:

"This is the disciple who testifies of these things; and we know that his testimony is true. And there are also many other things that Jesus did, which if they were written one by one, I suppose that even the world itself could not contain the books that would be written. Amen." (NKJV)

The only way they could stop Him from doing more as a man was to crucify Him. The marketplace must control their actions, especially how they respond in critical situations. Great ambassadors respond more than they react. When you chose to respond, it means you think through how you are going to act. Reactions are based solely on previous thought and judgment instead of present reality. Sometimes reacting is unavoidable, but most of the time it is. Every situation deserves a response, not just a reaction.

Before you react and put someone in their place, put yourself in their place and then consider your response. It reminds me of a story I heard as a young man many years ago:

A man in a hot air balloon realized he was lost. He reduced altitude and spotted a woman below. He descended a bit more and shouted, "Excuse me, can you help me? I promised a friend I would meet him an hour ago, but I don't know where I am." The woman below replied, "You are in a hot-air balloon hovering approximately 30 feet above the ground. You are between 40-41 degrees north latitude and between 59-60 degrees west longitude.

"You must be an engineer," said the balloonist.

"I am," replied the woman. "How did you know?"

"Well," said the balloonist, "Everything you said is technically correct, but I have no idea what to make of your information, and the fact is I am still lost. Frankly, you have not been much help at all. If anything, you have delayed my trip."

The woman responded, "You must be in management."

"I am," replied the balloonist. "How did you know?"

"Well," she said, "You don't know where you are or where you are going. You have risen to where you are due to a large quantity of hot air. You made a promise you have no idea of how to keep, and you expect the people below you to solve your problem. The fact is you are in exactly the same position you were in before we met, but somehow you have managed to make it my fault."

Funny story, but it illustrates a great point. Marketplace ambassadors may give information technically correct, but this begs the question, are the people still lost? People watch how you act and react in the marketplace as much or more than how you act at Church. Do your actions endorse your message or bring doubt and confusion? Your effectiveness depends on it.

Three Components Controlled Jesus' Actions

First, He had a plan. The Bible says we make our plans with the Holy Spirit's help and then God directs our steps. Proverbs 16:9. Too many want God's help, but have no plan of action. Do not be like the man who kept shouting to God for help. Finally, God shouted back, "With plans no bigger than yours, you don't need My help!" All marketplace ambassadors are called to great opportunities. Believe God for something bigger than you are and will outlast your lifetime.

Second, He formed a team. These men were human, and not divine, recruited from trees, back alleys, doctor's offices, fishing docks and tax collectors' booths. Some were educated and some were illiterate. Some had questionable resumes, bad attitudes, and moments of cowardice. However, Jesus taught them, trained them, set goals for them, and commissioned them as marketplace ambassadors. They went on to turn their world upside down. (Acts 17:6) Some of the greatest marketplace ambassadors are waiting to be recruited, but like the men standing around idle in the parable, they cry, "No one will hire us." For too long, the Church has actively recruited Ephesians 4:11 ministers for the pulpit without putting the same effort into recruiting Ephesians 4:1 ministers as marketplace ambassadors.

The Enemy has been eating the Church's lunch for 1700 years in marketplace recruiting. Look at the Kingdom's influence in business, government, and education. I think you will agree. Until the Ephesian's 4:11 ministers come to grips with the fact that, without adequately trained Ephesian's 4:1 ministers, the marketplace is not likely to change any time soon.

A Plan of Action

Third, He took action. He only had divine appointments. His Father ordered every step He took and every word He spoke. Should not our plan be the same? Why do we take job transfers and move half way across the country simply because it means a promotion and/or increased salary, without knowing it is best for our Kingdom assignment? Many marketplace ambassadors find themselves in a "country" without a calling.

God gives us a lot of room in making choices about life, but He gives us only one destiny. It is not so much geography as it is awareness of our Kingdom assignment and role as an ambassador. God never gives us an assignment that causes undo trouble for our families or ourselves. Yes, following God's plan for our lives, demands sacrifice and even pain at times, but never beyond His ability to bring victory. His plan is better than any other alternative. Actions without a plan, usually creates more sweat than significance.

II. The Ambassador's Profile

We find our key verse, I Corinthians 5:20, in the context of this entire Fifth chapter of Corinthians. In verses 1-8, we see Paul's confidence of Heaven. In verses 9-13, we see Paul's concern to please Christ. In verses 14-17, we see Paul constrained in his love for Christ, and in verses 18-21, containing our text (verse 20); we see his commission for life.

Our role as Christ's Ambassador in verse 20, must find its context in our confidence of Heaven, our passion to serve others through serving Christ, and being motivated in all we do by His love. As we consider the Ambassador's profile, we must take into account:

Most of the people we speak to have never visited our Kingdom.

Most do not accept the authority or even the existence of the King we represent.

The policies of our Kingdom seem to have little relevance for them and their current struggles.

Most will question our ability, as marketplace ambassadors, to express those policies persuasively.

Our Kingdom's Secretary of State, the Holy Spirit, opened and established our embassy in Jerusalem during the Feast of Pentecost in 33 AD. It is still open and our assignment is clear.

We are Christ's Ambassadors to our generation worldwide. There are no boundaries or limitations with our assignment. We have been empowered by our Secretary of State to represent our King and His Kingdom with all the rights and privileges that accompany that assignment.

Success is guaranteed and outcomes are certain. The manual for our assignment is still the world's bestseller and has been for centuries. It is current, relevant for any situation, and it accomplishes anything we assign it in accordance to God's will.

What is the profile (qualities) of those seeking to be marketplace ambassadors? What profile is the Secretary of State (Holy Spirit) looking for in those who seek to represent Christ in the marketplace? Without a doubt, number one is loyalty. II Corinthians 5:9-10 says, *"We make it our goal to please Him (Christ)...for we must all appear before the judgment seat of Christ."* (KJV)

The greatest pressure on any diplomat, on a foreign assignment, is immersion in the local culture. Many forget they are there to be a *different* voice. Marketplace ambassadors must never forget that before they have the right to be heard, they must earn that right by building relational equity with those they serve. Your right to be a marketplace ambassador comes with your assignment.

Your right to be heard is your personal responsibility. Unbelievers will never believe our message until we earn their trust. Jesus constantly earned favor with people *before* He spoke, via drawing water for the Samaritan women, feeding 5,000 hungry people on a mountainside, or cooking breakfast on the seashore for His most loyal followers.

There is a direct link between effectiveness and accountability. You may be praised or criticized by the natives, but it is the evaluation of our Secretary of State that matters. Eternity will not evaluate our work by an annual performance review, but it will test it by fire. If we forget this accountability, we are a disaster waiting to happen. II Corinthians 5:11 says, *"We know what it is to fear the Lord."* (NLT) This knowledge must set our priorities and guide our activities for life and marketplace assignment.

The second most important quality for marketplace ambassadors is integrity. We read in II Corinthians 5:11 *"God knows we are sincere, and I hope you know this too."* (NLT) The Apostle Paul says, "*What we are is plain to God, and I hope it is also plain to your conscience.*" He said this for two reasons. First, if any ambassador lacks integrity, (words and actions do not match); his presence will lower the reputation of the Kingdom in the eyes of the people to whom he is sent.

Second, the whole point of his mission is to build a bridge of trust through his communication and lifestyle. How many leaders do you know who, are blessed with outstanding talent and abilities, but you doubt their message because their integrity is questionable? Without integrity, you should "go home" before you are called home.

Humility is the third desirable quality for marketplace ambassadors. II Corinthians 5:12-13 provides the context for our role:

> *"Are we trying to pat ourselves on the back again? No, we are giving you a reason to be proud of us, so you can answer those who brag about having a spectacular ministry rather than having a sincere heart before God. If it seems that we are crazy, it is to bring glory to God. And if we are in our right minds, it is for your benefit." (NLT)*

People must have thought Paul to be insane. Has anyone ever accused you of that in your marketplace assignment? If they do, make sure it is for the right reason. Psychologist, Robert Jay Lifton, said in his book: "Destroying the World to Save It"

> *"Those who are consistent in their beliefs, who*

try to live according to a specific set of
principles, and who imagine that they have a
single core identity—are mentally ill."

Those called to be ambassadors in the educational arena must be up to the challenge. Liberalism has been tearing apart the very fabric of our Kingdom's values and ideology for decades. Two-hundred-fifty years ago, Christians dominated the field of education. The past 75-100 years have seen the Church's ambassadors pummeled by their peers and declared incompetent by their professors.

We must never forget that we represent Christ. Representing *our* Church, *our* denomination, *our* affiliation or us is not part of our assignment. It will take a "spirit of humility" when people set us up with the intent to destroy us. Nehemiah 8:10 says, *"...The joy of the Lord is our strength."* If you have no joy, you have no strength. If you have no strength, you have no humility (meekness under authority).

You will not succeed as a marketplace ambassador without humility. Humble ambassadors are not weak they are meek (power under control). If you are of the mindset that meekness is weakness, then ask Moses, how being the meekest man upon the face of the earth in his generation, worked for him. See also James 4:7-10 and I Peter 5:5-7.

The fourth quality desirable in a marketplace ambassador is spirituality. Kingdom core values must always be first. In I Corinthians 5:12, the Apostle Paul draws a very interesting contrast between two kinds of ambassadors. Those who take pride in what is seen by the public when the crowd asks, "What do you have to show for your efforts?" are one kind. This ambassador points to his achievements, driven by programs and numbers. According to their standards, Jesus was a dismal failure. If we take care of the depth of our marketplace influence, God and God alone will determine the width of our influence.

The second ambassador in verse 12, is concerned about what is in the heart, *"...having a sincere heart before God"* (NLT). Kingdom core values are this ambassador's primary concern. He is not concerned with the crowd's affirmation, only God's affirmation. He lives for one thing and that is to hear, "... well done my good and faithful servant" for all eternity. You can either "play to the crowds," or live a life pleasing to the One who called you to be an ambassador. Most of the time, it is difficult if not impossible, to do both.

The fifth quality of a marketplace ambassador is passionate love. I Corinthians 5:14 says, *"For the love of Christ constraineth us..."* Faithful ambassadors combine patriotic love for his home country with passionate love for the people he serves. The famed missionary, Joseph Damien, known as Damien of Molokai, so beautifully illustrates this kind of love.

The Hawaiian island of Molokai is one of the most beautiful islands in the world. Damien, a Belgian with a mission, left his homeland, not seeking a scenic place to live, but because his heart went out to the lepers who inhabited the island. All were expelled from their own lands in the Hawaiian Islands because families and friends feared they would catch the dreaded disease.

They knew nothing about a cure. Here in this beautiful setting lived those with this life-threatening disease, imprisoned by the world's tallest sea cliffs. To this day, even though the number with leprosy is few because of recent discoveries in medicine, you cannot just show up. You must have special permission to visit the island.

In this beautiful place, Joseph Damien laid down his life for those he loved. One morning as he was pouring boiling water into a cup 'for tea, the water splashed out of the cup and fell on his bare foot. Rudely awakened to the fact that the boiling water caused him no pain, he poured the boiling water on the other foot. It confirmed his suspicions; there was no sensation at all.

Fear gripped his heart as he realized his fate. As he went to the pulpit later that morning, he changed his opening line—he always began by addressing the congregation with, "My fellow believers." However, this morning he said, "My fellow lepers." He was now one of them. For years, he had given them hope for the future. Now he truly identified with their pain.

After he died, the Belgian government saw him as a national hero and wanted his body for burial in Belgium. The people of Molokai wrote the government asking for a part of his body as a memorial of his presence with them. The officials in Belgium cut off the right arm from his corpse and sent it to those who loved him so much, so they could bury part of him in the land he loved, among the people he literally gave his life.

Amazingly, even though leprosy desensitized Damien's sense of touch, it did not shorten his reach of love for the lepers of Molokai. When you ask converts to Christianity from any other world-religion why they convert, they will usually give you one of two common answers. Either there was an epiphany of Christ's presence or a Christian reached out to them with a significant act of love.

The reach of love works within the framework of one's felt need. One's felt need is seldom their real need. However, if you are going to reach the lost, that is where you must begin. Sermons always work best after reaching out in love to their felt needs first, but sermons alone cannot always do the job.

It is difficult to love people who continually reject your message. However, it is your demonstrations of love with unfettered motives that validates it!

Love will do more for a person who has never

experienced true love, than any theological debate or philosophical argument.

Love places no demands, but rather allows an opportunity for surrender to all of its benefits. Christ, came not to condemn the world, but to offer its lost souls the opportunity for freedom found no other way.

III. The Ambassador's Responsibility

We are ambassadors to a world in which our King has vital interests. If God had no word for those around us in the marketplace, we would not be assigned there, and certainly have nothing of importance to say. Nevertheless, God does have a message for those who touch our lives every day. We are His only voice and He trusts us with communicating His message accurately and consistently. Our motives and lifestyle must be pure. Our understanding about our responsibility must be clear and compelling.

In fulfilling our responsibilities, two things are required. We must first listen as one *under* authority and speak as one *given* authority. As marketplace ambassadors, listening as those under authority, our agenda and mission must be understood. II Corinthians 5:19 says, *"God has committed to us the ministry of reconciliation."* (KJV) Our agenda and message are given to us. We do not have the liberty to put our spin on it in order to make it more palatable. Jesus was sensitive to the culture around Him but responsive only to His Father who sent Him, no matter what His Father said about the culture in which he lived.

We must search the scriptures and listen for the voice of the Spirit, not for themes that please the audience and build self-esteem, but rather for direction and commands for war. When manipulating messages for best results, we risk becoming entertainers, popular maybe, but irrelevant at best and harmful at worst.

Second, marketplace ambassadors must speak as one given authority, not just talent and ability. All authority is given and never taken. The Centurion in Matthew 8 said, *"I myself am a man under authority with soldiers under me. I tell one to go and he goes. I tell one to come and he comes."* (NLT) The anointing always connects to our authority, not our ability. The ambassador who fails to speak the message he is given, is a dangerous distraction and an expensive irrelevance for the one he represents.

The message of marketplace ambassadors is one of responsibility. Mature ambassadors are attentive listeners and faithful speakers. They are consistent and concise in the messages they deliver. They must faithfully speak about four major themes:

First, they must speak about the one and only true God. Notice how many times God is mentioned in II Corinthians 5:18-21:

- Our entire message is from God.

- God is reconciling the world to Himself.
- God has committed the ministry of reconciliation to us.
- God is appealing to us.
- God made Christ to be sin for us.
- We are to be the righteousness of God in Christ.

Our ministry must be God-centered and people related—not vice versa.

Second, ambassadors must speak about Jesus Christ and not self. It is not enough to speak about God in general terms, but specifically what God the Father has done through God the Son through the power of the Holy Spirit. Scripture overflows with the certainty of Christ and it resonates with his Kingdom initiative. Conflicts abound at the mention of His name, with many who want to promote God, but deny Christ. If Jesus Christ of Nazareth is not God, very God, the Word of God as we know it is neither a reliable document nor a rule for faith and conduct.

This fundamental purpose is not about preference or hermeneutics, it is about, *"Neither is there salvation in any other: for there is none other name under heaven given among men whereby we must be saved."* Acts 4:12 (KJV). Peter, the great fisherman, turned headline speaker on the day of Pentecost said:

> *"If you be reproached for the name of Christ, happy are ye; but for the spirit of glory and of God resteth upon you: on their part (unbelievers) he is evil spoken of, but on your part he is glorified. Yet if any man suffer as a Christian, let him not be ashamed; but let him glorify God on this behalf."* I Peter 4:14, 15 (KJV)

Mohammad, Buddha and all other counterfeit gods, or so-called prophets of God, are neither equal to nor a replacement for Jesus Christ. Jesus Christ is in a league all His own. One day every person living or dead will bow their knee and call Him Lord. If we do not bow in this life, we will in the life to come. Marketplace ambassadors, who compromise this non-negotiable truth in their official capacity, must be recalled.

Third, ambassadors must not shy away from speaking about sin. God reconciled the world to Himself by *"No longer counting people's sins against them."* II Corinthians 5:19 (NLT) the way He did in verse 21. *"God made Him* (Christ—no one else qualified) *to be sin for us, so that in Him, we might become the righteousness of God."* Marketplace ambassadors cannot preach a gospel without sin any more than they can preach a gospel without Christ. Sin is the problem in the world and, sad to say, in the Church as well. Whether you violate God's word as a sinner or saint, the remedy is Godly sorrow that leads to repentance.

Fourth and last, ambassadors must speak about reconciliation and hope:

> *"What this means is that those who become Christians become new persons. They are not the same anymore, for the old life is gone. A new life has begun. All this newness of life is from God, Who brought us back to Himself through what Christ did. Moreover, God has given us the task (as ambassadors in the marketplace) of reconciling people to Him. For God was in Christ, reconciling the world to Himself, no longer counting people's sins against them. This is a wonderful message He has given us to tell others."* II Corinthians 5:17- 19 (NLT).

The Gospel (birth, death, burial and resurrection of Jesus Christ) offers far more than a self-help program or living a better life without transformation. It is the life of God invading the human soul and giving people new identity and purpose. It is about having the abundant life but not without forgiveness of sin, only Jesus Christ can give. As ambassadors, we must faithfully raise these core issues of one God, the need for Jesus, overcoming sin, and of reconciliation and hope without fear or compromise.

IV. The Ambassador's Goal

What are we trying to achieve and how do we measure our effectiveness? Our goal is establishing a good relationship between the King we serve and the Savior we love with the people He loves that are all around us. It is not the number of people we talk with, but faithfulness to the message that determines our effectiveness. The best ambassadors are many times, sent to the toughest situations. Therefore, the difference is not so much in the garden, but rather in the gardener.

Persuasion Not Manipulation

Ambassadors are always sent in the spirit of hope. In our text, Paul makes it clear that we must pursue our goal of transformation by means of persuasion and invitation, just as he urges Titus to convince the gainsayers in II Corinthians 5 and Titus 1. Do not leave the subjects of persuasion and invitation until people are transformed. I constantly see marketplace ambassadors trying to teach and disciple people who have not been transformed by saving grace, and empowered by the Holy Spirit.

Persuasion is more an art than a science. No matter how noble your message, how passionately you express it, without your ability to persuade others, the message goes unheeded. Again, we turn to our text, II Corinthians 5:11: *"It is because we know this solemn fear of the Lord that we work so hard to persuade others"* (NLT).

Queen Isabella of Spain rejected Columbus' petition twice to finance his voyage to discover the new world. He won on the third try. Why? He appealed to her need for gold, her desire to conquer Japan and her intention of spreading Catholicism. Instead, the lost Italian explorer discovered American and named the inhabitants Indians thinking he found India. Arguably, America became a global power instead of Japan because of the art of persuasion. According to Aristotle's *Rhetoric*, if you (ethos) are perceived by the listener (pathos) as having a message (logos) of good will, knowledge of your subject, and you have the best interest of your listener at heart, they will listen to what you have to say intently.

Whatever you call your success as an ambassador, that calling depends on your ability to persuade. Jesus knew that was true when He illustrated it by saying to a group of fishermen, "Follow me and I will make you to become fishers of men. And straightway they left their nets and followed Him." Mark 1:18 (KJV) That's persuasion!

As with anything new, you must overcome resistance and lack of interest. Ambassadors are persuaders – agents for change. You must believe in your cause and message. It is not about your slick presentation, but knowing as you speak the Word of God in faith; the Holy Spirit is preparing their hearts and minds to receive it. The Holy Spirit will not do it without us and we certainly cannot present a convincing message without Him.

Everyone is involved in the art of persuasion. The

new baby wants to be fed and his diaper changed. Try ignoring its persuasion efforts in the middle of the night. Teenagers want the keys to your car; ushers want you to sit in a certain seat; sales people want you to buy a certain product; and pastors want you to study God's word, pay your tithes and faithfully attend Church. No one does anything until persuaded. They will certainly not do it for the long haul or during times of crisis, unless fully persuaded in their hearts and not just their minds.

In our attempts to persuade men, the hearer should never feel manipulated. I do not want to feel like I am being used to fulfill another person's agenda or purpose, and neither does anyone else. Our efforts as ambassadors should never involve manipulating people against their will or treating them like just another "convert." Conversion to Christ is not a set of religious feelings.

A person becomes a Christian, when persuaded of the Truth of the Gospel and on that basis confesses Christ, not because of your forceful presentation.

> *"That if thou shall confess with thy mouth the Lord Jesus, and shall believe in thine heart that God raised him from the dead, thou shalt be saved."* Romans 10:9 (KJV)

If not careful, we can manipulate people to say things with their mouth, they do not believe in their heart. Abuses abound by immature, so-called evangelists and hard-driving immature Christians who pressure unbelievers with a relentless high-powered Gospel presentation, to make a commitment without a change of heart. People must understand with their minds, but unless fully persuaded in their hearts, they are not truly converted. The book of Acts overflows with the persuasive efforts of the Apostle Paul:

Acts 9:29—"...talked and debated with Grecian Jews."

Acts 17:2—"As was his custom Paul went into the synagogue and reasoned with them from the scriptures."

Acts 18:4—"Every Sabbath he reasoned in the synagogue, trying to persuade Jews and Greeks."

Acts 28:23—"From morning until evening he explained and declared to them the Kingdom of God and tried to convince them about Jesus."

I am not suggesting we can argue people to accept the Gospel message and thereby enter the Kingdom. However, no one comes to salvation without a clear presentation of the Gospel in terms he or she understand and made real by the Holy Spirit. Therefore, our first objective is Persuasion.

The second objective, after we have created a sense of urgency through persuasion, is closing our conversation with an invitation. *"We are Christ's ambassadors, as though God was making His appeal through us, we implore you on Christ's behalf: be reconciled to God."* II Corinthians 5:20 (NIV)

There must be sincerity and passion with persuasion. Supernatural understanding must fill our minds with the Truth of our message, and our hearts full of passionate love for the people to whom God has sent us. Without both, our efforts as an ambassador will have little effect, if any at all.

This is the mystery of sharing God's Word supernaturally. A man or woman speaks Truth from the Bible and things begin to move in the spirit world. The Holy Spirit reaches into the sin-hardened hearts of people with His inerrant and infallible Word through anointed vessels, and persuades them to accept His message of reconciliation. It is the only means available that changes lost men into "new creatures (new creations) in Jesus Christ." II Corinthians 5:17 (KJV) It is the greatest experience Christ's ambassadors can have.

Transformation, God re-forming man from the breath of His Spirit through His spoken word, as He did in the Genesis narrative and with His disciples in John 20, *"And he breathed on them and said unto them, receive the Holy Spirit."* He transforms fallen man through His word, now spoken by His ambassadors. What a privilege!

"If one died for all, then were all dead: And that he died for all, that they which live should not....live unto themselves, but unto Him which died for them, and rose again." II Corinthians 5:14-15 (KJV).

Marketplace Giant Killers

As ambassadors, we seek to persuade and invite people to accept God's message. We must never forget it's really God at work transforming hearts while we speak. Our job is clearing the bushes so they can see the cross. There are many great callings, but none greater than that of marketplace ambassador, delivering the message of hope, the Good News, and seeing lives redirected for the glory of God. Seeing people move from conversion to discipleship and then to warriors killing giants in the marketplace, is the payoff for all marketplace ambassadors.

Our job as ambassadors must go beyond believing God for converts to making disciples and reproducing giant killers. King Saul was not a giant killer so he could not produce giant killers. In the Old Testament, there were real flesh and blood enemies. However, as New Testament believers, we have but one fight and that is the "good fight of faith." I Timothy 6:12 (KJV) "Without faith, it is impossible to please God." Hebrews 11:6 (KJV) Ambassadors must live and walk by faith. If you have faith the size of a mustard seed, you will conquer every foe. Matthew 17:20 (KJV) The

Word of Faith must constantly fill our mouth. When we pray, we must pray the prayer of faith for things to move in the Spirit and manifest in real life.

We cannot teach and demonstrate what we have not learned and experienced ourselves. When we arrive at our assignment as ambassadors, we must have faith in the Government that sent us and faithfully proclaim its policies and positions that goes beyond rhetoric. It must tear down the enemy's strongholds and regain surrendered ground for extending the Kingdom.

5
RUNNING NOWHERE

The word idle, found in Jesus' parable of the workers in Matthew 20:1-16, may be far more significant than any originally thought. This parable teaches many lessons, but my focus is the word "idle" and its implications for the Church today.

All ministers of the Gospel, whether Ephesians 4:1 types, which are the doers or Ephesians 4:11 types, the trainers, have responsibilities relating to the marketplace as a whole. The Ephesians 4:1 ministers must execute their priestly duties with a kingly anointing when functioning within the marketplace. The Ephesian's 4:11 minister's assignment, which is neither more nor less significant, is equipping those same ministers for their specific marketplace calling.

For this reason, everyone who has answered the

Ephesian's 4:1 call has marketplace responsibilities that go far beyond the Church as an organization and meeting place, they include the highways and byways where people are living and working. It should not be a question of "either or" in regards to within or without the local Church setting, but "both and" for the Church to have prophetic impact where it is needed most—the marketplace.

In Jesus' parable, it seems the laborers were more concerned about their wages than their activity level. After 45 years studying the vineyard parable and observing the marketplace first hand, I find many ministers today far more concerned about finances relating to compensation for work, than bottom-line Kingdom activity associated with discipling the nations.

No matter when or where you enter the fields, the concern must be about the harvest of those fields as opposed to monetary gains surrounding the associated efforts. God will sort out the wage issues, in His own time and according to His own will. His compensation is always just and fair. This parable, as with His others, stresses God's unlimited grace, rather than earning God's favor.

The dictionary has a number of definitions for idle including, "not working or active; unemployed; doing nothing; of no real worth, importance or significance." The Greek word for idle in Matthew 20:6 is *argos* meaning, "Free from labor, at leisure, lazy, and shunning the work one ought to perform."

We must understand that the Church will never accomplish its assignment to "disciple all nations" without first having significant activity, presence and influence in the marketplace. While many in the organized Church, stand around idle in the marketplace, others confuse marketing the Gospel with evangelism. Simply put, they are not the same, but both are vital in their own right for expanding the Kingdom and making disciples.

Marketing is creating a sense of urgency and desire for whatever you are offering. Webster's definition of marketing is, "the act or process for promoting or moving goods from the manufacturer to the consumer." Webster's defines evangelism as "the winning or revival of commitments to Christ." The Church tries to create a sense of urgency for the Gospel through programs while unable to close the "deal" in the marketplace. Jesus not only created a sense of urgency, but also consistently won over new converts through His marketplace activity.

Some exceptions exist, but most of the Church today does not adequately prepares its members for evangelism or possess a clear strategy for preaching the Gospel of the Kingdom in the marketplace. No wonder most of the Ephesian's 4:1 ministers stand idle in the marketplace, as it relates to Kingdom expansion; they are ill equipped to be there. It is worth noting that Pastoral/Teaching type gifted leaders have dominated the Church world for the past 1700 years. They do not have the gift for equipping marketplace ministers for that task in particular, and they certainly cannot do it without the other Ephesians 4 ascension gift ministers. This simply ends up being a "one size fits nobody" rule that has never worked and never will.

Early Marketplace Strategies

Repeatedly, Jesus uses the terms "market" or "marketplace" yet the Church fails to comprehend how important they were to Him in laying the foundation for evangelism and discipleship. I am often accused of using too much business-type language in describing activities the Church must address in the marketplace. My response, "Keep in mind, this whole movement we call Christianity was started by a small business owner." He refused to get bogged down in the ecclesiastical system of His day, and I believe He went out of His way to avoid it. Jesus, His apostles, and especially Paul, were anything but idle in their marketplace.

The First Century Church altogether was anything but idle in the marketplace. From Peter's Day of Pentecost message, to the tragic deaths of the first team of apostles to the Diaspora of the Jerusalem Church, it was all about being active and effective in the marketplace.

By the third century, the Church's institutional

concerns began to take precedence over marketplace opportunities. The Church moved indoors and the religious managers found a way to take over and keep it there. A good friend of mine says the bird that flies in ever tightening circles eventually flies up its own orifice. Convulsion always produces self-protected systems designed to keep you safe and everyone else out. It became more about Church work in the building and less about marketplace activity in reaching unbelievers. Note what Jesus said in Luke 7:31-32:

"To what can you compare the people of this generation?" Jesus asked. "How can I describe them? They are like children playing a game in the public square (rendered "marketplace" in the KJV). They complain to their friends, "We played wedding songs and you didn't dance, so we played funeral songs, and you didn't weep."

For John the Baptist did not spend his time eating bread or drinking wine, and you say, "He's possessed by a demon." The Son of Man, on the other hand, feasts and drinks and you say, "He's a glutton and a drunkard and a friend of tax collectors and other sinners!" (NLT)

Jesus was describing the religious leaders of His day as children sitting around in the marketplace complaining to one another. They didn't have a clue who John the Baptist or Jesus was or why they came.

John abstained from the marketplace while Jesus was everywhere, yet they criticized both. If you continue reading, the writer establishes the idea that "wisdom is proved right by her actions." Ecclesiastes 7:23 (KJV) In other words, wisdom is proved wise when *life* is the product of the action. Both Jesus and John were at opposite ends of the spectrum, yet they both were life producers because of their people engagements. They were both on specific missions and both finished their course, which by the way, is rare among most. According to Matthew, it could be argued, the ends justified the means of engagement. You cannot justify your means if your ends do not result in life changes in the marketplace and beyond.

Ezekiel, the prophet, went to great lengths describing marketplace activities. Tyre was the center of economic activity and God's people were falling down on the job. Too many Churches are concerned with advertising what is happening inside the walls of their facility without concerning itself with what is happening in the real world. Advertising does very little to create activity in the marketplace.

Advertising should be a by-product of creating a sense of urgency in the marketplace, not the goal. Promote all the events you want, but until you do some direct marketing where it matters most, the Church will fail to see substantial and sustainable growth. Jesus and Paul did not hang out at the Church house. They intentionally went to where the lost are found. They were by no means idle in the marketplace. They used Church meetings for their intended purpose, teaching and training Ephesian's 4:1 ministers for their marketplace calling.

Making disciples should be a way of life, not an event. The reason why we have to have events surrounding evangelism today is because people have become ineffective and passé concerning the expansion of God's Kingdom on earth. Too many are waiting for the "Rapture Bus" with their bags packed and ready to go. We must consider carefully the words of King Solomon; "... but he who sleepeth during harvest is a son who causeth shame." Proverbs 10:5 (KJV)

Marketing searches out the person or group that needs to be reached. Evangelism communicates the message marketed in a way that can be heard. Discipleship completes the transaction. Most of the time, the Church is idle in the marketplace because the pastors and teachers have everyone at the building in services and activities that feed their gifts, but do little to create activity in the marketplace. Oh, there is the occasional plea for reaching your friends, neighbors and co-workers, but seldom does it have top priority.

Then we have those who call themselves evangelists, but rarely do you find them in the marketplace sharing the Gospel and contending for the faith. Most go from church to church as revivalists, teachers, exhorters, prophets or "music-narians." Anyone with a traveling ministry is lumped into a group we call evangelists.

The Church not only needs revival, it needs brains. She desperately needs solid, balanced and Biblical teaching by those called, gifted and anointed for marketplace ministry and the EQ (Emotional Quotient or Emotional Intelligence) necessary for helping people grasp it. If evangelism, if done correctly, produces activity in the marketplace—not just overflow crowds at churches and sports arenas.

A true evangelist is someone who preaches or shares the Gospel with those who never heard, like Philip in the book of Acts. Could it be those we call evangelists and struggle keeping their schedules filled, have misidentified their gift? Maybe they should do as the Apostle Paul; start bringing value to the marketplace by getting a job and letting God use them in the marketplace.

True evangelists are passionate about sharing the Gospel with those who have never heard it. They always generate marketplace activity and usually without the fanfare or Church testi-phoney to prove it. Some of the most gifted evangelists never travel from church to church, ever. Their ministry schedule is full with hardly any opening. We call it marketplace ministry and most who find their ministry there are well paid.

Most churches would be better to train the evangelists God gave them, sitting in their services every week, and quit looking for someone to stir up the saints to do the work of evangelism, but never engaging the marketplace for his or her self.

Jesus gave five gifts to the Church when He ascended and evangelist was included. Paul told Timothy, the pastor, "Do the work of an evangelist." Of the five gifts in Ephesians 4, only one is the responsibility of everyone in the Body of Christ, the evangelist. When the entire Church, including its leaders, takes this responsibility seriously, you will see activity in the marketplace.

The target must be the harvest fields of the marketplace, not the pews of the Church building. Everything taking place at the facility called the Church should be about preparing laborers (Ephesians 4:1 ministers) for the harvest. We call it "God's House" because it is dedicated to His work, not because He lives there. He is only there because he comes with us when we attend. Believers and unbelievers alike seem confused about where God lives.

There is too much emphasis on getting people "active in Church." This usually means finding a place to serve at the Church doing Church work. There is not enough emphasis given to being the Church, and doing the work of the Church in the marketplace. It is like having an army and getting all the soldiers active in basic training, but never going to battle or learning how to shoot a weapon.

The purpose in both cases is not to make basic training more exciting, but preparation for the battles to come. The local church is where we are supposed to get commands for war. Both are necessary, but neither should take precedent over the other.

Most of the Church stands idle in the marketplace because they simply don't know what to do. Just as the workers in the parable stated, "No one will hire us." Many laborers are in the fields, but most do not have the spiritual awareness of what is going on around them because they have not been taught how to listen.

Most are not prepared, trained or coached for their assignment relating to Mark 16 or Matthew 28. Their lives are divided between sacred and secular resulting in idleness in the marketplace. They are taught a mindset of either/or as opposed to both/and. Most cannot see a direct connection between what they see and hear on Sundays and how it relates to what they do in the marketplace Monday through Saturday.

Traditional Church models and leaders need to change that or the marketplace remains idle and the laborers unemployed. The motor's running, but the car is going nowhere.

6
THE SECULAR VS. THE SACRED

God has a purpose for you and your business much greater than profit, providing jobs, customer satisfaction, or even sales. It is to glorify the Lord of the Harvest in the marketplace—your place of ministry.

Until marketplace believers influence all three entities controlling every nation, we will never "*disciple all nations,*" in the way the Lord instructed His Church.

We must infiltrate and allow God's favor to elevate us until we have superior influence in the marketplace, government, and educational institutions. The Church, through the five-fold minister's model (Ephesians 4:11) must provide teaching, training and coaching that results in better-equipped disciples and marketplace ministers.

We must stop compartmentalizing our lives between what many see as "the secular versus the sacred" mentality. That separation does not exist in God's world nor has it ever existed for that matter. Your life is the integration of all the God-given opportunities around you woven into a seamless life lived to the glory of God, regardless of what you are paid to do. These opportunities encompass both the church world and the marketplace; there is no difference.

If God has called you to the marketplace, government service, or education, you must find God's purpose for being there and act on it. Your destiny is making a difference for the Kingdom, not having a job to meet your needs or a career to prepare you for retirement. Our work is what we do *while* fulfilling our call, not *until* we fulfill our call, no matter who you are or what you are doing.

You can approach your business, job or marketplace opportunity as a Christian in three ways. First, you can see yourself as a Christian in a secular business or position. Second, you can operate or work in a Christian business in the secular marketplace, or third, you can have a Kingdom business or position related to Kingdom purposes and committed to Kingdom expansion.

Your business or position in the marketplace exists for many reasons, but it exists primarily to glorify

God and live for the "Five Greats" developed in the first chapter.

The Great Commandment in Matthew 22:35-40, based on love.

The Great Commission in Matthew 28:18-20, based on obedience.

The Great Opportunity in John 4:35, based on discernment.

The Great Disturbance in Acts 1:8 and 2:4, based on passion.

The Great Day in I Thessalonians 4:13-18, based on eternal hope.

The target must be the whitened harvest field ripe for picking, not the well-padded pews of a local church where the *already picked* fruit many times sits and rots. Christians should not have to take time off or retire in order to enter full-time ministry. My business or position *is* my ministry.

Our business or position in another's business is not our total ministry any more than my "Church work," or what we do at the local Church building, the sum total. Because of this convoluted mindset, too many are so busy doing church work they have neither the time nor energy for the "work of the Church," which takes place *outside* the facilities of the local Church during the rest of the week.

Fundamentally, the terms "bi-vocational" and "part-time minister" are each an impossible oxymoron. We should have one calling that is lived out in every area of our life, and not just six to eight hours a day. Where is the church today? The church is wherever His sanctuaries (you) are located because as the apostle Paul said, "*We are God's building.*"

We do what we do regardless of the location of our calling. We must do it on purpose, with passion and specificity as an extension of who we are. Ministry should be an outflow of the organic nature of our personhood and not a task we perform for money. We see throughout the biblical narratives this extension of all those whom God called;

"Adam where are you?"

"Moses what are you doing here?"

As with Gideon, Joshua or the Apostle Paul, we must seek God for our purpose, find a voice for doing it, and fulfill our destiny. Effectiveness, regardless of endeavor or effort, is about relationships. The Bible says our whole life, was planned before we were born and our steps were ordered of the Lord for His service. If that is the case, how can we have both secular and sacred parts to our lives or Churches?

This kind of thinking has created more chaos than community, within Christ's body, than nearly anything else. Even the world notices it, and its two-faced result has done more harm than good in most instances. This was never God's intension—it was never His plan. We must never forget what the Bible says about the Nicolaitans, when discussing the division between Ephesian's 4:1 and 4:11 ministers. "But this thou hast, that thou hatest the deeds of the Nicolaitans, which I also hate" Revelation 2:6 (KJV).

And "So hast thou also them that hold the doctrine of the Nicolaitans, which thing I hate" Revelation 2:15 (KJV).

What were the deeds of the Nicolaitans and doctrines of the Nicolaitans? The Greek roots of this compound word are *Nicho*—and *laos* "conquer" or "up against" and "the laity." A group of people who thought they were better and different from the rest.

Specifically, they developed this ungodly concept of the division between the clergy and the laity which thing God HATES, just like He HATES the division that is divorce as seen in Malachi 2:6.

See—http://www.angelfire.com/la2/prophet1nicola itans.html.

Nicolaitans, a first century sect, which anticipated Rome's priesthood by dividing God's people into an unscriptural clergy-laity relationship.

Worship & Lifestyle Excellence

"Jesus doeth all things well." Mark 7:37 (KJV). Our significance, as well as our success, should be linked

to a spirit of excellence. We obviously do some things well and even some things with excellence, but the goal of every Christian is to catch the *spirit of excellence* that develops into a *lifestyle* of excellent living. Moreover, we should never strive to be perfect through the exterior motivation to please men, but rather through a humble heart quick to obey our Master's voice, admit our mistakes, and please our Lord.

Excellence is the inspiration behind all great leaders for the simple reason that the spirit of excellence is the inner passion to do our very best with every opportunity, bringing glory to the Lord, regardless of our calling in his Kingdom.

Excellence is not an option or a goal; it must be an essential way of life. I Corinthians 10:31 reads, *"...whatever you do, do to the glory of God."* This doesn't mean doing a *secular* duty in a Christian way, but rather, offering up to the Lord *everything* we do as a sacred and sacrificial offering to the Lord, not out of compulsion, but our own free will.

He is always worthy of our best efforts, regardless of the task or whom it is for. Somehow, many have adopted the idea that ministers work for God, but everyone else works for the world, but nothing could be farther from the truth.

Our ministry (our business, job or position in life) should reflect this spirit of excellence. Our sales should be honorable and effective. Financial affairs should be honest and without question. Profit performance should be outstanding, reflecting our Kingdom commitment and the favor of God. Our technology should be current, innovative and appropriate.

Our employment practices must be exemplary while the size and scope of our business or position-impact is ultimately up to God. However, the standard by which we operate and the fervor we function in must be high and without compromise, this goes for laborers, owners, pastors, plumbers, apostles and homemakers; there is no difference.

One purpose of our business or leadership impact is creating and distributing wealth for the expansion of God's Kingdom. Wealth was God's idea and has been since He created the world. Someone once said, if the wealth of the world's resources (timber, minerals, land, manufacturing, etc.) were sold on the open market, it would make every person on this planet a billionaire six times over.

God created value and wealth at creation and He gives His children the power to gain it, use it to establish His covenant and extend His Kingdom on earth (Deuteronomy 8:18). Too many people believe God for miracles when He is saying, "Go to work!"

The Hebrew words for work and worship are very similar. God's intention was that our work would be our worship and our worship would be our work. Worship, by its definition, must be more than a song offered in the local Church house or behind closed doors. Worship is a lifestyle as suggested by Paul in the Roman letter. Living out the perfect (mature) will of God in our daily lives (outside of the local Church building) becomes our reasonable *act* of worship to Him (Rom. 12:1-2).

Many of us have been bamboozled into believing this can only occur in a "worship service" led by a qualified worship leader or pastor, but this line of thinking robs us from the beauty of holy living as the Psalmist says in Psalm 29; "Worship the Lord in the beauty of holiness." (KJV)

The Theology of Work & Business

The Genesis 1:26-31 passage provides a fundamental theology for work and business that deserves our full attention. Business should never be a means to an end. Adam and Eve had the task of managing God's creation after instructed to "subdue" and "make use of it," which teaches us that God is always about creating value and filling needs. This should cause you to expand the potential God has put in you so you can determine your own value within the marketplace. Adam and Eve were not only given management responsibilities, they were to master (dominate) all of God's creation. Their leadership potential was to create a bright future for all His creation and not just themselves.

In Genesis 1:31, God decrees all his work "good" and thus valuable for all to enjoy. It was only *after* the Fall that fallen mankind corrupted everything, including God's original business model. God never condemns business, only corrupt business people. Why did God include a business model in creation, if He did not intend for man to use it? The business model was God's original design for human functionality, within a system of exchange for goods and services.

First, to create wealth as a means of providing for Kingdom citizens, called to Kingdom building and expansion. He could have provided a steady stream of miracles and provisions, i.e., ravens, cruse of oil, manna in the wilderness, water from a rock, turning tap water into wine, money in a fish's mouth and feeding 5,000 men plus wives and children from a little boy's lunch. Instead, He chose to do most of His providing for humanity through the natural means of work (the original sowing and reaping model), which is supposed to be our worship to Him, not a drudgery to avoid or retire from. Many avoid work simply because they do not understand its purpose within the scheme of God's Kingdom.

Second, business creates relationships whereby God can display and demonstrate His grace in and through the lives of those devoted to Him. The Ephesians 4:1 ministers (those living out their lives worthy of the *general* calling) many times are able to be in places the Ephesians 4:11 ministers (those gifted to equip those with the general call to the

world *although not better than them or more special*)
may not be welcome, gifted or called to serve.

Third, business was part of the New Testament
Church. When you understand that the Holy Spirit
was not sent to be a laborsaving device, but rather a
labor-enhancing partner, work takes on a completely
new meaning. Lydia, the merchant in Acts 16, was a
beneficiary of the ministry of the Holy Spirit in the
marketplace as was James and John the fishermen,
Luke the physician, and Paul the apostle. In fact, I
believe Paul's ministry never really took off until he
created value in the marketplace with Pricilla and
Aquila in Acts chapter 18.

Fourth, Jesus was a small business owner most of his
life and He recruited His first team for world
evangelism from the marketplace.

Six entrepreneurial women provided most of the
support for His three-and-a-half-year itinerant
ministry as I stated within the premise of this book.
Today's church will only see impact in the
marketplace, government, and education in direct
proportion to the value they bring to those arenas on
a consistent basis. Impact comes from Ephesian's 4:1
leaders developed by Ephesian's 4:11 leaders into
Disciples of Christ: called, committed, and
empowered as "Kingdom Builders" fulfilling their
God-given call seven days a week.

I am often asked what I think is the number one

hindrance to world evangelism. After four-plus decades of ministry in the church and the marketplace, I answer without hesitation; the division men have created between clergy and laity, sacred and secular, full-time and part-time. This classification is the mind-set of many Christians and traditional church leaders and, in fact, in the plan of the Accuser of the Brethren.

None of these classifications is Biblical or recognized by the Holy Spirit. Even a cursory study and elementary understanding of scripture, reveals God's original intent and continuing desire for a kingdom of priests, delivering the Gospel with Holy Spirit fervor to the entire world, resulting in the discipling of entire nations. Note: I Peter 5 and Revelation 2.

We need to develop a Biblical theology for ministry, where Christ is Lord of the Marketplace, that encompasses business, governments, and education, not just the organized Church. May I dare say that Christ is not really Lord of many local Churches? That may be why He is not Lord of the marketplace, the educational, and government arenas where their Church is located ninety percent of the time.

Ephesians 4:1 says, *"Therefore I, a prisoner for serving the Lord, beg you to lead a life worthy of your **calling**, for you have been **called** by God"* (NLT). I believe this applies to all ministers, not just those in the Church structure. Those with Ephesians 4:11 gifts, called out of all called ministers for equipping Ephesians 4:1

ministers for the work of the ministry where God has placed them, not just for church work where they attend.

You understand this well when you contextualize the *"saints"* of Romans 1:7, because they set the pattern for Romans 12:1-2 and Ephesians 4:1.

All called ministers were *"...created in Christ Jesus to do good works, which God prepared in advance for us to do." Ephesians 2:10* (KJV). The implications should be obvious. First, they were prepared in advance without the input or approval of man. Second, they are for us to do, and not just meet and talk about. Third, He has given all called ministers everything needed for life and godliness, and not to just a select few.

Because of this fact, we should not stop short in teaching the priesthood of all believers and the need for a fully empowered priesthood in the public sphere where most Christians live out their lives and where the greatest Kingdom battles are fought. Allow me to elaborate with three specific principles, which are these: Your ministry should not be bi-vocational; your Kingdom business or position must have purpose and be intentional; and, your business should be a relational enterprise.

I. Ministry should not be bi-vocational.

All of life is sacred for the Christian. Someone once said, "When is a bird most glorifying to God, when it is flying, singing or when it is preaching?" Answer: what glorifies God most is not the essence of the activity we do, but whether it is what He wants us doing now. What you were made to be and designed to do is your calling. All Christians have a God-given destiny, but few know or understand what it is. Romans 1:7 says, *"To all in Rome who are loved by God and called to be saints…"* Literally, "saints" mean *"holy ones."*

Every Christian is consecrated and set apart for God's purpose and calling. Tie this to Romans 8:28, *"…called according to his purpose,"* and you have a formula for understanding better the idea that you have one. We must stay focused on the unlimited application of God's call and not the limited application that comes with today's ministry model. All Christians, by definition are *called* Christians, or they are not Christians at all. Being sanctified, holy and acceptable is not the call or status of a select few "special" believers, but the mandate for everyone in the Body of Christ.

The call is always *to* something and *for* something, not just a one-liner on your business card or so you can get a better parking space. That something is your destiny, not just your service to the Body of Christ and witness in the marketplace. Consequently, your destiny will always be bigger than you are and it will inevitably outlast your lifetime. If not, maybe what you have is only a position, title, business or a passionless pursuit you call a job. Each calling is just as significant as every other calling. The idea of degrees or levels of calling are a breeding ground for depression, division and pride.

This is why Paul instructed the immature believers in his first letter to the Corinthians not to compare themselves among themselves. If God has called you to business, government, or education, no other calling would be a promotion, but would be a step down. After all these years, I am still trying to understand what people mean when they say they are quitting their job and going into "full-time ministry."

II. Your Kingdom business or position must have purpose and be   intentional.

Your life's calling must have purpose and a sense of mission beyond making a profit and consuming more earthly goods. God is a God of purpose. Everything He ever did, He did on purpose. Scriptures abound that support this premise, i.e. Genesis 1:26, Jeremiah 29:11, Romans 8:28-29 and Ephesians 1:11, just to name a few.

Your business exists to glorify God, not you. It exists to contribute to major Kingdom building activities that support His purpose and not just your personal ambition. If you are an owner or an employee, your efforts must bring glory to your God first. Man's idea of business is to simply gain wealth and control others. Man did not create business, God did. God instituted it with the Divine purpose of edifying humanity thus ultimately bringing glory to his Creator.

How do you discover God's Kingdom purpose for your business? Look and learn from the scriptures filled with the directives on how to do this. First, we must submit ourselves to God and those He puts in authority over us, not to rule over us, but rather to be "helpers" of our joy. Then God will reveal His will to us who willingly act on it and understand the following three concepts.

A. His purpose revealed in his Word.

"The secret things belong to the LORD our God, but those things which are revealed belong to us and to our children forever, that we may be able to do all the words of this law." Deuteronomy 29:29. (NKJV)

"He has shown you O man what is good. And what does the Lord require of you but to act justly, to love mercy, and to walk humbly with your God?" Micah 6:8. (NKJV)

"All scripture is God-breathed and is useful for teaching, rebuking, correcting and instructing in righteousness so the man of God may be thoroughly equipped for every good work." II Timothy 3:16-17 (NLT)

"His divine power has given us everything we

need for life and godliness through our knowledge of him who called us by his own glory and goodness. Through these he has given us great and precious promises so, that through them you may participate in the divine nature and escape the corruption by evil desires." II Peter 1:3-4 (NIV)

B. The knowledge that God's will for your business is revealed when He knows you are ready, willing, and obedient to His word, His will and His way, not just committed to being a good businessperson.

God will not reveal His will to those who want to know what it is before they decide if they want to do it. They must follow a clear path in fulfilling God's destiny for their life and ministry, which is submission without reservation, revelation through His Word, and clarity of the next step. It is obedience without question that determines the manifestation of His will arriving on time.

This was Paul's point in Romans 12:1-2. We must understand God's general will for humanity and His specific will for our own life. We must surrender and embrace it with passion. As we go through this process (not an event), we will change and conform to not only His image, but also His will as well. We will have understanding, wisdom, and knowledge through the opportunities and experiences only He can provide.

Our steps are ordered of the Lord and not random occurrences without purpose. We are not victims of circumstances, but we are more than conquerors through Him. Too many trust God in Church services, but try to do it on their own in their business, job or Kingdom position.

C. The purposes, plans and will of God are spiritually understood.

The purposes, plans and will of God do not always make sense to the natural mind or feel comfortable to the flesh. If you want to know what the *"hope of your calling"* is for your life and business, develop the following disciplines in your daily walk.

First, pray. Prayer is not so much a matter of position, as it is the attitude of your heart. Prayer is not a scheme that we use to influence God to allow us to have our own way. It is not a tool we use in order to create a particular outcome, but rather a means of communication with the Father. Neither is it a scream where we are trying to get God's attention so we can inform Him of our situation as if He did not know.

It is not a one-way monologue where one person does all the talking. As we pray we understand, not just the will of God, but also the heart of God. What comes *from* our heart always goes to His heart. What comes from our mind seldom reaches the ceiling.

Second, read, study, memorize and confess the Word of God for the right reasons. Live a life saturated by

149

the Word of God. The Truth of God's word not only sets you free from sin, but also frees you to understand God's purpose and plan for your life and business. The facts of life are true, but they are not always the Truth. Truth always overrides the facts.

It is not "you shall know the facts and the facts will make you free," but *"you shall know the truth and the truth shall make you free."* John 8:32 (KJV) It is one thing to be set free (an event) from sin and its effects, but quite another to be made free (a process) to know the heart of God and all that He has planned for us before we were even born.

Third, hang out with balcony people and avoid basement people. Balcony people have an elevated view of life. They can see a long way and look over a lot of stuff from that perspective. Basement people cannot see very far, the view is cluttered with things hindering them from seeing what God has for them including their loved ones and their marketplace opportunities.

Solutions, find some balcony people with a Kingdom business outlook, know their calling and use their business to extend God's kingdom. You do not find these people hanging out in the basement, be it in the Church or marketplace—both places have basements you must avoid.

Fourth, be a reader. Readers are leaders. Stay informed about what is going on around you, in your world and the rest of the world. The sons of Issachar *"understood the times and knew what to do."* God is at work everywhere all the time and He wants you to know what He is doing, why, and how you and your marketplace ministry should be involved.

Fifth, keep a journal. All great leaders are writers even, if not published. They record the significant events and activities of their lives. Putting your thoughts on paper helps crystallize what God is saying to you and reveals how you really feel about it.

Sixth, have personal mission, vision, and value statements. If you do not understand God's specific purpose and plan for your life and how these statements help you fulfill the destiny He has planned for you, you will never be all you can be and accomplish all He has planned. You may have a level of success, depending on how hard you work, but you will never have real significance. That only comes through a close relationship with your King. Success is what man says about you. Significance is what God reveals to others about who you really are.

III. Your business should be a relational enterprise.

A wonderful friend of mine has a statement that has become his mantra within his consulting business and his life; *"Relationships are primary, not instrumental."* Leadership and ministry (your business) is about relationships. You cannot have a successful one without the other. However, it must go beyond products, goods and services if it is to have Kingdom impact. Scripture is clear about the importance of building relationships in ever-widening circles and spheres of influence, known today as the network.

From the beginning, God created humanity for fellowship and relationship with Him and his fellow man. He called Israel out of all the nations for this very reason—to form a relationship with Him and then extend it to others. He created them to have a special covenant relationship with Him. All believers are called out of darkness and grafted into the family of God for the purpose of relationship.

Few things of significant value are accomplished outside of real and honest relationships. Those who serve you and your business interests must feel some sort of relationship to you. If not personally, at least to the vision you have established. If not, as a leader you have failed them. Those with poor relationship driven opportunities will not be as productive as they could have been.

Relationships are not only vertical and horizontal; they should be ever widening circles. They should include family, friends, competitors and even enemies (enemies help keep you focused). Relationships are fundamental to life—we have them whether we want them or not and thus, we should always strive to make them better. Family relationships are different because we do not choose them, but we must endeavor to develop them into life-giving moments when we can.

Covenant relationships run deeper than any other kind. Most are developed through divine purposes as was David and Jonathan's, but all covenant relationships are built upon friendships that are closer than family—"There are 'friends' who destroy each other, but a *real* friend sticks closer than a brother." Proverbs 18:24 (NLT) Because of the nature of "real" relationships, they have the power to provide Kingdom opportunities when viewed by others.

The spread of the Gospel never happens effectively through organizations and institutional efforts, only through the individual efforts by members of those organizations. It is when we live out our faith, through these *authentic* relationships, that purposes and divine pursuits begin to happen.

The Great Commission is also about relationships. You cannot warm people to yourself, win them to Christ and develop them to be disciples without being real (authentic), relational, and relevant. If you lead a successful and significant business, you understand the importance of real relationships with your core leaders, team leaders, vendors, customers, and stakeholders. In this wise, everything about the Kingdom is relational as well. Develop relationships with people, not just for business reasons, but also for the purpose of winning them to Christ and helping them to be better followers—known as disciples. You will find that when relationship is the goal, and not getting them to Church, you will usually have opportunity to invite them to some Christian endeavor as a result. Everyone wants to buy, but nobody wants to be sold.

So now what? Communicate the Truth as the Holy Spirit provides inspiration and direction. Teach, train, and coach new believers to deeper levels of Kingdom life and effectiveness. Equip the mature believers for the work of the Church as well as Church work by helping them develop their God-given gifts and talents.

Finally, release the trained, equipped and empowered to their Kingdom assignments. Location of the assignment makes no difference if the assignment is business, government, or classroom of higher learning. Your business or professional position *is* your calling. Do not allow yourself, or others to devalue your calling. Allow God to use you, your business and your influence to strengthen and extend his Kingdom wherever you find yourself.

7
THE GREAT DIVIDE

Why do we use un-biblical terms when referring to manmade divisions of Christians, such as the called, the non-called, full-time, part-time, bi-vocational and others? Someone asked me a few years ago the number one reason for holding back world evangelism and seeing entire nations discipled. Without hesitation I responded, "The non-biblical tradition of dividing believers into clergy and laity and forming a ministry class system."

Many church professionals are uninformed about the terms clergy and laity, how they started and the way they have contributed to idleness in the marketplace. If you truly believe and practice the priesthood of all believers, as the Word of God teaches, you will eliminate them and the confusion they have caused. These terms and their implications are long-standing.

traditions promoted widely throughout the church world and will not go away easily. Nevertheless, they must go, if idleness is eliminated in the marketplace. The root words for these terms are found in the New Testament, but how they have been used since the third century, cannot be found in the New Testament whatsoever.

Clergy and Laity

The English word "clergy" is rooted in the Greek word "kleros." It means "a lot or an inheritance." In 1 Peter 5:3 the elders are exhorted not to lord it over "the lots" referring to the entire flock of God. Nowhere does the New Testament use any form of "kleros" to designate a separate class of ministry leaders. Instead, it uses the term "clerou" found in Colossians 1:12 and Acts 26:18. The saints, which are the body of Christ, are seen as a collective whole, God's inheritance throughout the New Testament. We have done great harm in the church and created idleness in the marketplace by referring to a separate class of people as "clergy." This has inadvertently excluded everyone else from the ideas of effectiveness and responsibility when it comes to Kingdom advancement.

The English word "laity" is rooted in the Greek word "Laos," meaning people of God. The Greek word "Laikos" meaning "laity" is not found in the New Testament at all. Regardless of what title you choose to use, the five-fold gift minister, bishop, elder, deacon and pastor within the body of Christ are *all* the "Laos," the people of God. There is however, a slight distinction between the ministers in Ephesians 4:1 and those found in Ephesians 4:11 as discussed earlier.

Where It All Started

Where and when did these terms begin? Most historians agree it began when Constantine became Emperor of Rome around 325-50 AD. He bought his way into the church when he saw the church could not be defeated. He thus joined it and either started or greatly reinforced the clergy-laity division and it has been a profound hindrance ever since. Clergy designated a limited number of ordained individuals thus giving way to the idea of "special."

They were set apart to handle the liturgical elements and programs of the church respectively. When those individuals are set apart, by implication, everyone else is set aside. I believe this contributed greatly to the church being set up for failure not only within its own walls, but also in the marketplace most of all.

With any brand of or commitment to a liturgical model of ministry, regardless of how small that commitment is, becomes a contributing factor to idleness in the marketplace and a dysfunction within the model. One of the worst doctrines to come from this church model is when there are no clergy present; there can be no distribution of the sacraments (water baptism, communion) or clear presentation of the Gospel.

Ignatius (AD 110) was probably the first to dispense this model of doing church as is clear from his writings:

> "Indeed, when you *submit to the bishop as you would to Jesus Christ*, it is clear to me that you are living not in the manner of men but as Jesus Christ, who died for us, that through faith in his death you might escape dying. It is necessary, therefore—and such is your practice that you *do nothing without the bishop*, and that you *be subject also to the presbytery*, as to the apostles of Jesus Christ our hope, in whom we shall be found, if we live in him. It is necessary also that the deacons, the dispensers of the mysteries [sacraments] of Jesus Christ, be in every way pleasing to all men. For they are not the deacons of food and drink, but servants of the Church of God. They must therefore guard against blame as against fire" (*Letter to the Trillian's* 2:1–3 [A.D. 110]).

> "In like manner let everyone *respect the deacons as they would respect Jesus Christ*, and just as they *respect the bishop as a type of the Father*, and *the presbyters as the council of God* and college of the apostles. *Without these, it cannot be called a church*. I am confident

that you accept this, for I have received the exemplar of your love and have it with me in the person of your bishop. His very demeanor is a great lesson and his meekness is his strength. I believe that even the godless do respect him" (ibid. 3:1–2).

Little if any of the present-day models of church and church leadership existed for the first 300 years of the Churches existence. Yet the Gospel was able to spread through the known world primarily through evangelizing the marketplace. The fact these terms exist and are continually promoted shows a total disregard for what Jesus Christ had in mind for world evangelism and church function.

This not only undermines the canonical accuracy of scripture, but also creates a secular mindset in ninety five percent of the co-laborers producing idleness in the marketplace. This mindset not only strikes at the heart of the priesthood of all believers that Jesus paid for, but also greatly reduces effectiveness in the marketplace overall.

Since Constantine, the clergy-laity divide slowly grew through the centuries until firmly entrenching itself throughout most of the church world today. Now the heretics and radicals are those who believe, preach, and practice the priesthood of all believers with few exceptions. Presently, most Bible schools, colleges and seminaries teach and give mental ascent to the priesthood of all believers, but function in the manmade liturgical system as a way of life.

Two of Christ's ascension gifts in Ephesians 4, pastor and teacher, dominate most institutions that provide training for future church leaders. Just as the Genesis narrative teaches us that everything reproduces after its own kind, seminaries today are not exempt from this principle. Any leader can teach, train and coach, but only reproduce who they are.

Whomever God made you is what you will reproduce. You cannot reproduce who you are not. Pastors and Teachers produce other pastors and teachers regardless of the curriculum they use and the learning opportunities they provide. You may teach the theory, but you only reproduce who you are through on-the-job training.

Pastors and Teachers cannot reproduce and develop apostles, prophets and evangelists. Every person God gifts with an Ephesians 4 ascension gift can and must develop others who have the same gift, but are undeveloped and immature. Gifts of any kind do not come fully developed. It is naïve and often dangerous to allow people to operate in a gift that is not mature or lacks training.

Another tragedy this clergy-laity divide creates is discouragement at best and total burnout at worst in people trying to fulfill impossible expectations for a role called pastor, especially when they do not have the necessary gift for that calling. Success and significance in ministry is not caused by title, position, seminars or training when trying to flow in an area in which you are not gifted. I have heard it said, "I would rather burn out than rust out." Both statements lack wisdom, are emotionally immature and poor role models for new ministers, regardless of calling.

Ministerial Burnout

You can burn out flowing in a gift given by the Holy Spirit because unfulfilled expectations still bring life's greatest disappointments. Burnout comes from trying to fulfill unreasonable expectations of yourself and others through human wisdom and wrong models of operation. God's expectations of us are never more than we can bear. God's word guarantees it. You never overcome the lack of a gift through training, seminars, seminary degrees or more perks. Either you have it or you do not.

If you have a five-fold gift, who besides you knows it because it takes one to know one. If you do not, faking it will not help. Many ministers today try to fake it until they make it, but never make it and the body suffers through their experiment. Working harder will not fix this problem. Praying harder will not fix it either. Changing locations will not help you overcome this conundrum although it may alleviate the local church from having to go through this.

Submit yourself to a wise person "over you in the

Lord" Hebrews 13:7 and 17 and be content with what you *are not* for once. Knowing who you are is great, but knowing who you are not is paramount for both you *and* your hearers. God has a place for you where you will fit like a hand in a glove. He has gifted you for that place and only that place.

If you are frustrated, unfulfilled and struggling, you can be sure all those around are as well. We must remember the words of Paul, "But God has placed each member within the body as it has pleased *Him*." Many are not pleased with His decision and will try to circumvent, but this is not helpful or healthy for anyone.

"Clergy", "pastor", "senior minister", etc., whatever term you want to use, comes with expectations that you have all the responsibility and all the answers. You are compensated to do whatever it takes to keep the ministry growing. If the budget allows you, hire more professionals "to do the ministry." The laity, if they have time, is there to help the Ephesians 4:11 ministers fulfill their calling. This strategy is bogus.

Burnout, shrinking morale, divorce, addictions, and suicide are common among the Ephesians 4:11 ministers. Statistics are unbelievable among the group we call clergy. God never intended one group to carry the entire responsibility for His work and the rest help if their schedule and time permits.

The present ecclesiastical system needs to be

scrapped in favor of the Biblical mandate in I Corinthians 12:14 *"....the body has many parts, not just one part..."* (NLT)

This change, if it comes, will happen slowly. Those with the most to lose become the defenders of a system that cannot be supported scripturally and thus become the major contributors to idleness in the marketplace. Those in both traditional camps, clergy and laity, must be willing to take the criticism that goes with any paradigm shift.

Both groups must lead the way to actions that will result in marketplace ministry as Jesus intended. Idle, secular-minded "lay people" must become the Ephesians 4:1 ministers God originally proposed. They must change from *just* having a job or career to Kingdom ambassadors with a passionate God-given destiny.

Flattering Titles

Many in the clergy camp over the last five years have shared their hesitation with me about making substantial changes. Some have an outright fear of losing their status while others fear losing honor, influence or the ability to lead if the non-clergy join the ranks of those called to real ministry and no longer serve only in supportive roles.

However, this is an unwarranted fear. If we are true ambassadors then we must leave the halls of self-focus and convoluted ministry designed to promote and protect self and enter the real world ministry of Jesus and His disciples. We must update the hermeneutical gap for relevance sake, but we must quit what isn't working.

If you are concerned about losing your leadership influence because your title changes, you have little if any, influence now. Your leadership ability is not linked to your title or position, regardless if elected, appointed or inherited. Title authority is killing us just as it kills in corporate America as well. Authority is nothing more than the fruit of responsibility within your God given area of expertise. The more you are elevated in the Kingdom, simply means you get a bigger mop bucket.

Your ability to lead effectively and with honor is due to your God-given gift and not your ability, not your title on your desk and door or your certificate on the wall. "For I know not to give flattering titles; in so doing my maker would take me away" Job 32:22 (NIV). Scripture is clear in Hebrews concerning those who are over us in the Lord:

> *"Remember them which have the rule over you, who have spoken unto you the word of God: Whose faith follow, considering the end of their conversation. Obey them which have the rule over you, and submit yourselves for they watch for your souls, as they must give an account that they do it with joy, and not with grief: for that is unprofitable for you."* Hebrews 13:7;

17 (KJV)

If you are an Ephesians 4:11 minister, you will have no problem with those you lead if they understand and value the gift God has given you. Most of the trouble begins when we start pushing titles, offices and positions without reflecting a servant's heart. Without a servant's heart, you should not be in leadership no matter what gift you have or how strong you think it is. When we always introduce ourselves by our title and or position I wonder, "Who are we trying to convince, ourselves or everyone else?"

After 45 years of developing leaders and building teams in the church and marketplace, I have found the biggest problem is emotionally immature leaders. They do not understand their gift, never developed it or are simply out of place. As President Regan told Russian Prime Minister Gorbachev, "Mr. Gorbachev; Tear down this wall!" The Berlin Wall that continued to separate East and West Germany for decades. I believe God has been saying for centuries to the Church, "Tear down this wall of separation between clergy and laity."

We are all citizens of one Kingdom ruled by one King. There are different gifts, talents and abilities, but all have been called, gifted and empowered. Ephesians 4:11 ministers need to teach, equip, train and support their Ephesians 4:1 ministers' efforts in the marketplace. Apostolic gifted leaders will do that without question. Pastorally gifted leaders tend not to provide such help and are consistently challenged.

Idleness in the marketplace will vanish when this wall is removed and with it any kind of a ministry class division. We must maintain with all due respect the distinction between Ephesians 4:1 marketplace ministry calling and the Ephesians 4:11 five-fold ministry calling.

Let's end the misunderstanding at best and the costly division at worst between the two equal but separate callings. If we do not address this issue, idleness will continue to dominate in the marketplace.

8
THE THREE MARKETPLACE REALITIES

If the Church is going to lead and produce activity in the marketplace, she must understand at least three marketplace realities.

First, leaders must lead according to the times and not according to tradition.

> *"And the sons of Issachar, men who understood the times, with knowledge of what Israel ought to do."* I Chronicles 12.

All the men listed in I Chronicles 12 came in full battle array to Hebron with a single purpose, to make David the king of Israel. However, according to the text, it seems only the men of Issachar knew what to do. So many want to lead, but have no understanding what is going on around them much less in the rest of the world. If they are informed then few know what to do about it. Leadership is much more than information and knowledge alone; you must know what to do next.

Our nation and the entire world for that matter are facing many challenges, but without Divine intervention, there are no answers. Issachar and his two-hundred men faced a challenging moment in the life of Israel, but God gave them divine revelation on what to do next. May He do the same with the leaders of our nation as they face challenges never seen before in our nation and a world growing smaller and more complex every day.

More important than whom is president of the United States is, how effective are Christian leaders in the marketplace, government and education? What is the biggest factor surrounding the ability of a ministry or organization having long-term influence and prophetic impact in the three entities controlling every nation? I'll tell you what it is not; not an outstanding mission, vision, or value statement, not the latest information and communication technologies, not even access to unlimited ministry tools, time and money, as helpful as all of them would be.

I believe the most important asset, is the ability to hear the voice of the Spirit, follow His strategy, and develop a passion to innovate and adapt as He leads during these challenging times. We need a keener sensitivity to His voice, not only for our nation, but also for the Church as a whole. While most in the Church have maintained a strong allegiance to the Inerrant Word of God (The Map), we have lost our sensitivity to the compass (the Holy Spirit), compasses and maps go together.

If we are going to maximize the opportunities the Church has today in the marketplace, we must develop and mobilize leaders at all levels of ability, talent and gifting. They must "understand the times and know what to do." They need to function effectively at all levels of leadership opportunity and challenge in the Church and the marketplace.

If we are going to lead according to the times and not traditions, we must have the courage to invest all available resources; money, good will, energy, facilities and ministry tools in new and innovative ways, without abandoning the best of yesterday. It is naïve to think we can carry all the baggage of yesterday into the tomorrow God has planned for us and still be successful. Wise and courageous leaders know the difference between the best of yesterday and traditions harmful for today's reality.

The men of Issachar knew the difference and knew what to do about it. They knew how to take yesterday's best, combine it with today's opportunities and create marketplace effectiveness many only dream about. The things today's "men of Issachar" must know, understand and execute are; knowing the difference between leading and managing your ministry or marketplace effort; setting goals for your innovative ideas and understanding today's and tomorrow's leadership and management realities. If you do not understand the difference, most likely you are a manager. As I said previously, managers are leaders by influence, but find it difficult, if not impossible to create a compelling vision others want to follow.

Managers are doers and leaders are visionaries, and both are vital for creating marketplace activity. Managers are about efficiency, procedures, and coordinating the bureaucracy. They keep us on the right path today while providing little, if any, direction for the future. They tend to limit imagination and creativity while slowing progress and critical change. However, today would not happen without them.

Leaders are visionaries. They dream about how the future can be. *"Behold the dreamer cometh...let us kill him...and we shall see what will become of his dreams"* Genesis 37:19-20 (KJV). Be careful with whom you share your dreams; and remember, you are not a leader without one. If you do not have a dream, you should be managing someone else's. When the elders' in Moses' day did not have a dream of their own, God placed the same Spirit Moses had upon them, so they could help support Moses' efforts.

Visionary leaders base their vision on at least two things, innovation and inspiration. Innovation is based on wisdom, knowledge and understanding inspired by the Holy Spirit. It is causing resources and influence to flow to those who add value and away from those who do not. A sense of mission, vision and passion for living for a cause greater than you inspires people. Innovation and inspiration always increase stakeholder value. Just as today's success will not happen without great managers, tomorrow's vision will not happen without great leaders.

When talking about innovative goals for ministry in the Church and marketplace consider the following, Great leaders always foster ministry renewal. Too many wait until conditions demand something must be done, but smart leaders always consider, what to not only do, but also how to do it well. Great leaders make significant changes before they must, while at the same time knowing just when to act on those changes. Good leaders make changes before things get out of hand. Poor leaders resist change and many times cannot read the handwriting on the wall. They try making changes no longer necessary and have little or no impact on the future.

Great leaders constantly inspire their team to make innovation part of everyone's passion. They are in a constant state of war against the status quo. Challenging the process is not an occasional event, but rather a way of life. Innovation is not resisted, but valued and embraced by every leader at every level. Great leaders cultivate and develop a creative ministry environment that lasts while creating solutions that work.

> *"So it is with effective leadership. The leader whose thinking is constrained within well-worn ruts; who is completely governed by his established passions and prejudices; who is incapable of thinking either grey or free; and who can't even appropriate the creative imagination and fresh ideas of those around him is as anachronistic and ineffective as the dinosaur. He may by dint of circumstances, remain in power but his followers would almost certainly be better off without him."*
> —Dr. Steven Sample, President USC.

One of the two biggest traditional threats to this kind of creative and innovative environment is, "We've never done it that way before." A close second is, "What's in it for me?" Great leaders constantly and firmly resist these traditions and insist their team members do the same.

Leaders who lead "according to the times and know what to do;" understand today's and tomorrow's leadership and management realities. They understand that information and communication technologies are a lot like the Internet, available to just about anyone in the world. These leaders are transparent, with few, if any secrets. They are reliant on personal integrity; knowing that a lot of personal financial gain is at stake and they ensure the right relationships stay connected. Leaders who do not understand this reality will find their ability to lead effectively significantly challenged. Marketplace leaders understand this certainty while church leaders are still catching up.

Understanding our times and helping those we lead know what to do should be at the top of every leader's prayer list and active agenda. We must get them ready for eternity, but at the same time ready them for tomorrow.

The world is busy trying to help people cope with today's challenges. Dr. Phil, Ophrah, and many others seem to have the answers, but we know better. God help us as leaders, not only help those around us cope, but lead them on a mission to be "more than conquerors through Jesus Christ our Lord" in the home, the church, and in the marketplace. The greatest challenge for those who choose to lead, according to the times and not tradition, is the ability to enlarge our thinking while being led of the Spirit to respond with courage and conviction to the best ideas. The Sons of Issachar did, Jesus did, why not you?

Prophetic Impact in the Marketplace

Second. The second marketplace reality that the Church must understand is how to have appropriate prophetic impact through Ephesians 4:1 ministers. Marketplace ministers (Ephesians 4:1) have made a substantial difference for decades with little or no affirmation from the accepted, traditional five-fold gift ministers (Ephesians 4:11). The cause has been a lack of understanding rather than an intentional rebuff. There are exceptions, but not enough general acceptance given the challenge in the marketplace harvest field. This harvest field houses those who generate and control the world economy, governments and educational institutions, which is why it is so vital that an impact is made.

Marketplace ministers are not representatives of the five-fold gift ministers, but rather they are the result of working in tandem with one another. Prophetic impact in the marketplace requires understanding and partnership on the part of both groups of ministers; each has an essential role to play. The command in Matthew 28 goes unanswered without the synergy created when both groups understand their own call and role.

It's high time the Church, via marketplace ministers, steps up and provides the prophetic impact that creates the tipping point and will be remembered. I have seen evidence in the marketplace of all Ephesians 4 ascension gifts in my 45 years of marketplace experience. There are leaders who have an apostolic gift; others have that of the prophetic, pastor (shepherd), teacher or evangelist. The fear of titles and offices has greatly weakened or sometimes even eliminated the effects of these gifts in the marketplace.

The Church will have far more impact scattered than it will gathered if she understands her Kingdom mandate. We must never abandon the exhortation to "Not forsake the assembling together," but remember all the reasons for that gathering. One is equipping the saints (Ephesians 4:1 ministers) for the work of the ministry that has direct connection to the (Kingdom) marketplace. We tend to forget the context of the writers intention; the days were evil.

Prophetic impact goes beyond providing informational teaching; there must be a prophetic declaration that redeems, transforms and brings people into a life-changing relationship with their Creator. Prophetic declaration creates and maintains a sense of urgency for extending the Kingdom, not for swelling the membership rolls and attendance figures of local congregations.

Prophetic impact involves marketplace ministers living and sharing the gospel *"as one having authority and not as the scribes."* Mark 1:22 (KJV) Prophetic declarations always challenge and echo freedom for the masses held in bondage because of satanic deception while providing Divine strategies for moving people from despair and hopelessness to a life filled with hope, peace and true joy.

Prophetic gifted marketplace ministers are hope-dealers not purveyors of gloom and doom. It was the message of hope Jesus came preaching that produced true repentance and transformed lives. At the same time, prophetic declaration does not ignore sin and all its forms of evil invading every segment of the marketplace. There must be no compromise or lack of clarity in our declaration of the Kingdom message if it's going to make a difference in people's lives.

No issue is untouchable regardless of the financial costs, attendance or lack of political correctness. 2 Timothy 2:15 must be the foundation for all marketplace ministers:

> *"Be diligent to present yourself approved to God, a worker who does not need to be ashamed, rightly dividing the word of truth"* (NKLV).

The Greek word *spovdazo* (diligent) is also translated *study*. It means, "Be very active," implying intimate acquaintance with the Author that provides mature understanding and revelation. The King James translation is misleading here; many think that simply studying their bible will create this desired result, but this is not true.

We are encouraged to "make every effort to present ourselves to God," which then positions us for that revelation. What good is bible study if we are not actively pursuing His desire for us to be more like Him?

Correct or Politically Correct

If we *have "been given all authority in heaven and*

earth" (Matthew 28:18), we must give diligent preparation for that role. Many have been given significant opportunities only to fail and "turn back in the day of battle" like the Tribe of Ephraim in the Old Testament. Too many high-profile ministers, in both groups of ministers, have a world platform only to compromise and fail to give a prophetic declaration in the name of political correctness.

Jesus said the Gospel would be an offense, but the messenger should never be offensive (e.g. Jonah). Nonetheless, the only way to have prophetic impact in the marketplace is deliver an uncompromising message. If we say, we really love the lost; we will not compromise the Truth, the only tool that sets people free.

Many confuse prophetic impact with being an idiot. They think the more they offend, the better things are. This is short sighted and insecurity driven. The *only* people Jesus offended were religious. Nowhere do we see Jesus offending the world; we only see Him loving it. The marketplace is not looking for a Church; they're looking for a place to be loved.

Many in the marketplace are not looking for the Truth, as we understand it, they are looking for an experience that changes their present circumstance and gives them a reason to live. No one had greater prophetic impact in the marketplace than Jesus did yet the religious saw Him as compromising. I suspect it is because no one loved the lost more than He did.

He was constantly building relational equity with those the "church" of His day rejected—sadly, not much has changed. He spent time with them. He went to their homes, parties, funerals and many other life events. He was there when they needed Him most. He was comfortable with them because he knew who He was. Their lifestyle neither threatened nor intimidated Him, with which one I am sure He did not agree. Sinners where comfortable with Him because they knew He really loved them without judgment or criticism.

Many today would never set foot in a bar or attend a festive event for fear of being dirtied, but Jesus was famous for this, which was why they (religious leaders) called Him a drunk. The church has confused "be ye separate" with isolationism and thus we have limited our effectiveness within the lives of those who need Christ the most.

They received his message because he loved them so much and they knew it. The Church's prophetic impact in the marketplace will be in direct proportion to its love commitment in the marketplace not how loud we deliver the message.

John the Baptist confronted the evil and religious spirits of his day. He called people to repentance and holiness, as was his mandate. His life was such an example many confused him with the Messiah to come. His message had credibility because of the life he lived. It worked because this was his destiny. It was the Baptist's job to draw a line between action and mere talk. Can we do or be any less in our generation and marketplace opportunities if God calls us to do so?

There is a price to pay for prophetic impact. When we confront the cultural evils of our day, there is always a cost. Dan Cathy, CEO of Chic-Fil-A Restaurants, knows the price of having prophetic impact in the marketplace. The truth of "All that will live Godly shall suffer persecution." II Timothy 3:12 (KJV) is beginning in the United States and will only increase.

Many who spoke up for God in Hebrews 11 ended up being stoned, imprisoned, mocked, tortured and crucified. It is happening now to our brothers and sisters in restricted nations around the globe. How many, especially in the West, are willing to be "blessed" according to Matthew 5:11-12, *"bless them which persecute you, revile you and say all manner of evil against you falsely for my sake?"* Yes, the cost for prophetic impact is great, but the payoff far greater. Let us not be *"idle at the eleventh hour"* in the marketplace.

Third. The third marketplace reality that the Church must understand is the World is our parish. If the Church, not the organization, but the ecclesia, the called out ones, fulfills its mandate *"...make disciples of all nations"* (Matthew 28:19), I believe the following four adjustments must take place as the Church views the world is its parish.

First, our ministry philosophy must change from traditional to biblical. Terms such as clergy, laity, part-time, full-time, called, secular, and bi-vocational have contributed to the inability of the Church to see the discipling of entire nations. God never intended for these divisions and distinctions to exist. Especially in light of his desire for the priesthood of all believers described in Exodus 19:6; I Peter 2:5,9 and Revelation 1:6.

His desire has always been a Divine partnership for Kingdom expansion made clear in Ephesians 4:1. The text declares all Christians called to full-time service as New Testament priests, regardless where that sacred service takes place. Ephesians 4:11 speaks of the "called out ones" from those in Ephesians 4:1. With clear instructions, they must equip the 4:1 ministers for the "work of the ministry" in the field of service where God has called them.

Second, our ministry mindset must change from church planting to Kingdom expansion. True church planting is always a by-product of Kingdom expansion in the three entities that control every nation. They are the marketplace that creates all wealth and drives the economy, governments that pass laws and regulations for maintaining order, and educational institutions that determine the values and philosophies of every generation. Too often, we plant churches and then try to create the demand. Only passionate Ephesians 4:1 ministers answering a divine call and seeing the world as their parish can effectively create that demand.

Creating a sense of urgency is what marketplace activity should be all about. Overcoming idleness in the marketplace is not taking on all the cultural flashpoints by debating whether it is Christian or not. We have enough religious pundits willing to staff those debates. Jesus never allowed Himself to be drawn into those discussions. There never seems to be any winners, only compromise.

Jesus showed us how to operate in the marketplace. He was always busy with appointments set by His Father. You could find Him in the marketplace, drawing water for an outcast, feeding five-thousand hungry men with a lunch hardly enough to feed a boy, healing the sick by the hundreds or turning water into wine. He did not have to tell people who He was; he just demonstrated it and that with ease.

Ephesians 4:11 five-fold ministers must teach, train and send Ephesians 4:1 full-time ministers into these ripe harvest fields with a Kingdom mindset, not with an American motivation to increase wealth. They need to infiltrate by divine call, elevate by divine favor and eventually dominate these controlling entities, via their influence as salt and light by Divine power. Then the Church has the responsibility of conserving the results of these ministry (not secular) efforts by planting local congregations to do it all over again.

Third, our ministry leadership model in every local congregation must include all five leadership gifts mentioned in Ephesians 4. Then one anointed leader can provide the opportunity for the other four to operate in a spirit of cooperation not competition. Excellence must prevail in teaching, training and execution of these gifts in an atmosphere of love and faith. Many claim the title and office, but the impact of their gift is less than desirable.

Leadership in the church and marketplace is not about the authority to command, but rather a passion to serve (Mark 10:45). Great leadership is about influence not command and control. What you cannot accomplish through relationship and influence will never happen through appointed, elected or positional leadership.

Christ's ascension gifts in Ephesians 4 provide oversight to the gifts of the Holy Spirit mentioned in both the Corinthian and Roman letters. They will help every local congregation manage the present and provide leadership for the future in the Church and marketplace. They are as vital to the success of the twenty-first century Church as they were to the first century Church. Their intended use is just as much for the daily marketplace as for the Church meeting on Sunday. They were not for the exclusive use of the five-fold Ephesians 4:11 ministers in the Church arena, but also for the Ephesians 4:1 ministers doing spiritual warfare in the whitened harvest fields.

Fourth, the leadership team must know how to provide strategic leadership not just management functions. Pastor (the gift) by definition is a manager as a shepherd manages sheep. The pastoral gift shepherds and cares for the flock. Someone must know how to create a compelling vision for the future and that requires a different gift.

All management problems are simply indications of previous leadership failures, i.e., the BP oil spill, closed churches and defeated leaders. Only apostolic leadership gifts can address those issues effectively.

Strategic leadership is all about change. Discipling a nation requires greater leaders not better managers. Great leaders make changes when they do not have to; good leaders make them when they have to; and poor leaders are selling tickets after the train has left the station. If allowed, the managers of every generation make the rulebook thicker and reigns of authority tighter.

They debate style, form and process. They discuss the past, debate the present and sometimes argue about whose interpretation of the future is correct. All of this does little in changing our world significantly. We need good managers because they bring order to the vision strategic leaders create. However, better management alone will never influence and disciple a nation. This demands strategic leadership whose job is creating synergy for change around a constantly changing landscape.

If the world is our parish, if the Church's command is sending full-time gospel ministers there to make disciples; then we must understand we cannot manage our way there. The Church must develop strategic leaders who know how to disciple the faithful while developing future strategic leaders in every generation for the marketplace, government and education.

Organizational leaders must seize the moment and inspire those they lead to fulfill these once-in-a-generation opportunities. The world is always one generation away from being evangelized and discipled, if that generation sees the world as their parish and not confine their ministry efforts within the walls of a local church facility.

As Jesus commanded Lazarus loosed from his grave clothes, Ephesians 4:11 ministers must loose their Ephesians 4:1 ministers from the traditions that have long hindered world evangelism and entire nations from being discipled.

The more the Church understands these marketplace realities the more prophetic impact it will have. Without this understanding and commitment to change marketplace culture, we risk repeating outdated and failed attempts at reaching the world Jesus came to save. I invite you to become the marketplace leader your peers and coworkers are dying to see.

9
WHY THE MARKETPLACE AND WHY NOW

Why the marketplace? Why did Jesus, first century Church leaders, and especially the Apostle Paul put so much emphasis and effort in the marketplace? They probably did because the marketplace touches everyone who lives regardless of where they live. Either directly or indirectly, even in the most remote areas, what happens in the economic centers of the world affects everyone.

It plays a part in every society and people group. It affects every political system, military power and historic era from Cain and Abel to present day centers of power on Wall Street, London, Beijing, New Delhi and Tel Aviv.

Consider the Athenian markets of Paul's day, the silk

trade routes of Marco Polo, the gold mines of Africa, and the oil fields of the Arabian Peninsula. They have one thing in common, people seeking to trade goods and barter services in order to earn money to survive and someday, thrive and climb the social ladder. All hope to enrich and transform their lives and those of their loved ones. Only those who have more than they need to survive are able to give and to support the expansion of the Kingdom.

Jesus, always drawn to the marketplace, was at home with business owners, tax collectors and women entrepreneurs. In Matthew 9, He attended a dinner hosted by Matthew, former tax collector, a brand new convert and now a faithful follower of Jesus.

On another occasion, He went uninvited to the home of a crooked tax collector by the name of Zacchaeus. Zacchaeus had heart change, made 400% restitution to those he had ripped off and then Jesus pronounces a blessing on his home. A group of entrepreneurial women supported Jesus, a small business owner and His team of marketplace types (Luke 8:1-3).

Many of the stories and parables Jesus shared had a marketplace flavor. One story told of a marketplace leader who gave various amounts of money to three individual investors and came back later for an accounting (Matthew 25:14-30). Two doubled their money and were highly commended for their efforts.

The third, out of fear of losing his "seed," buried it in

the ground and was chastised for not investing it wisely. The first two saw sound investment opportunities and increased while the third waited for the perfect opportunity that never came. Everything about the Christian life is about increase, whether it is personal growth, souls or finances.

Marketplace Leaders Are a Gift

Marketplace leaders (Ephesians 4:1 ministers) are a gift to God's Kingdom work just as much as Ephesians 4:11 five-fold gift ministers—Apostles, Prophets, Pastors (shepherds), Teachers and Evangelists. If the marketplace is impacted, it is because these two groups of ministers find a way to honor and affirm each other's gifts to the Kingdom. Each has a clear God-given assignment to fulfill.

For centuries, marketplace ministers, regrettably known as laymen, were marginalized and overlooked as a gift of God given to enhance and extend His Kingdom around the world. As a result, Para-church groups have sprung up to address the heart cry of many marketplace leaders who know they are called to minister—not just support those who do.

These marketplace ministers need to be recognized, affirmed and included as vital partners on the world evangelism team. Many who struggle in finding a place on Ephesians 4:11 ministry teams are not called to be on that team. However, because of the Church's failure to recognize and affirm their gift and calling, they desperately try to make it happen because they lack an understanding of their call within the marketplace. There should not be classes of ministers in the Kingdom—only different assignments and locations of service. Church leaders must not fail in their efforts to be sincere and consistent in praying for God's favor on all their marketplace ministers' efforts and ministry.

Kingdom success is determined by how well Ephesians 4:11 ministers teach, train and coach their Ephesians 4:1 marketplace ministers to win every day. Jesus believed this evidenced by how much time He spent with His own marketplace team. He totally ignored the ecclesiastical system of His day when laying the foundation for His Kingdom. The Church can no longer afford to ignore the greatest resource at her disposal: Ephesians 4:1 ministers and the marketplace where they spend two thirds of their lives.

Why the marketplace? Because that is where the first and final battles for the Kingdom are fought. Every major religion and political power that exists and ever existed knows that to win you must control the world's resources in the marketplace. Any student of world history knows that fundamental fact. While the twenty-first Century Church seems confused or hesitant about having prophetic impact in the marketplaces of the world, the Apostle Paul never shared this same concern.

Using today's traditional Church vernacular, Paul would have been at best a bi-vocational minister and at worst a layman. The local ministerial association certainly would not have credentialed him. He made no apologies for his pedigree outlined in Philippians 3 and II Corinthians 11. He was from the tribe of Benjamin, a Hebrew of Hebrews. Concerning Jewish law, he was a Pharisee, a practicing attorney.

When Jesus knocked him off his horse on the way to his hometown of Tarsus, he was going there with an open arrest warrant for any Christian he could find. When it came to living by the law, there was none better—he was faultless. Yet everything he learned in the religious system of his day he counted as nothing. None of that would be of any value in the calling God had on his life for the marketplace.

Paul was a tentmaker by trade, choice and calling. He did not go to the marketplace in Acts 18 because he was broke, needed employment or because he was a failure in the religious system of his day. He went there because of what was going on in his world at the time due to the growing Roman Empire, the convergence of cultures and marketplace demands.

The Pax Romana (Latin for "Roman Peace") lasted from 27 BC to 180 AD. There was relative peace, prosperity and stability throughout the world during that time. There were no major wars or unrest even though it may have been forced pacification as some historians describe it. Public services greatly increased including the building of the Apian Way (Roman road network) and other engineering marvels of that day. A single language, Konine Greek, prevailed over the empire. Travel throughout the empire was easy, and trade greatly increased. All of this was conducive to the rise of Christianity.

Apostle Paul Was Not Bi-Vocational

Paul was born in Tarsus, raised in Jerusalem, trained by Gamaliel and Jewish by faith and culture. Tarsus was a prestigious and wealthy city, one of the top two or three university cities in the region. It was a confluence of cultures along with his upbringing and training that helped shape his personality and leadership style.

He was among the educational elite, probably in the top two or three percent of his class—maybe one of the reasons he was a prolific writer and used by the Holy Spirit to write at least thirteen books in the New Testament. Along with the advantage of Roman citizenship, Paul leveraged all this in his call to the marketplace and the missional life-style he lived there.

How and why did he work in the marketplace when he could have easily made a superior living practicing as an attorney? Paul probably worked for many reasons, some obvious, some not. Primarily I believe he worked in the marketplace because it was his call and enhanced his ability and opportunities to spread the Gospel. There are so many ministers frustrated trying to fill pulpits that would be much more effective as ministers in the marketplace. They would be more fulfilled and their families would be much happier and blessed. I don't know where the idea came from that in order to be a called minister; you don't have to work anymore.

Paul did not work in order to survive or because money was scarce; he worked because he liked it. He mentioned in one of his letters that people that eat were people that worked. I am not saying that in order to be an effective leader you have to hold down a job, I am saying that holding down a job does not mean you are not an effective leader.

Paul's work was not a distraction to his call it was part of it. It was an essential part of his calling. He did not see his life as being divided between totally dedicated to Christ and building God's Kingdom. There certainly were no secular versus sacred distinctions in Paul's life and there should be none in ours.

Let us look at some Bible passages that describe Paul's approach to marketplace ministry. *"Or is it only Barnabas and I who have to work to support ourselves"* I Corinthians 9:6 (NLT). It could refer to Paul and Barnabas supporting themselves on a mission to Cyprus and Galatia. *"And when I was with you...the brothers from Macedonia brought me all I needed. I have never been a burden to you and never will"* II Corinthians 11:9 (NLT).

Paul worked so as not to be a burden, but also allowed others to help with his needs. Other passages such as I Thessalonians 2:9 and II Thessalonians 3:8 speak of *"working night and day."* and not eating without paying for it as mentioned above. At the same time, Paul makes a very strong argument defending the right to be supported by the recipients of his message.

Why he chose not to seek their support, I do not think can be proven conclusively. In my life and ministry, I have had it both ways, but never felt one was superior or more spiritual than the other was. Paul must have felt his convictions lined up with his calling. I doubt he felt conflicted about how the Lord provided for his personal needs and missionary journeys.

Too much is made over who is in full-time ministry, part-time or bi-vocational (splitting your ministry with a secular job in the marketplace). This distinction has led to unwarranted judgments as well as poor behavior towards young ministers who give their heart and soul while acting in both models.

Unfortunately, many in paid ministry positions today are no more anointed than I am an astronaut, but because many cannot distinguish between calling and charisma, the show goes on. Paul thus lived by this one amazing rule, *"This one thing I do,"* no matter where his call led him.

Personally, I believe Paul's ministry took off in Acts 18. In verse 3, he becomes partners with Priscilla and Aquila in a tent making business. This gave him a platform for ministry while bringing value to the marketplace. An interesting observation is that although Priscilla and Aquila were employed in the marketplace, they had a profound impact on Apollos, a native Jew from Alexandria who was "mighty in the scriptures."

> *"Meanwhile a Jew named Apollos, a native of Alexandria, came to Ephesus. He was a learned man, with a thorough knowledge of the Scriptures. He had been instructed in the way of the Lord, and he spoke with great fervor and taught about Jesus accurately, though he knew only the baptism of John. He began to speak boldly in the synagogue. When Priscilla and Aquila heard him, they invited him to their home and explained to him the way of God more adequately" Acts 18:24-26 (NIV).*

In verse 4, he reasoned with Greeks and Jews in the synagogue on the Sabbath. In verse 5, Silas and Timothy came from Macedonia with financial support, but that did not stop him from continuing his marketplace ministry while conducting business.

From Acts Chapters 18-20, we can conclude that Paul did not consider tent making, preaching and teaching, planting churches and missionary journeys mutually exclusive. He allowed others to contribute toward his efforts, but not as his primary support. Many times Paul not only provided for himself, but for those on his team as well.

The Consummate Marketplace Leader

Paul modeled what should be the model for the vast majority of all Christians who have marketplace responsibilities assigned there by God to fulfill their calling and ministry. Paul worked in a very anti-Christian environment, as bad as or worse than we have today. If you cannot model the Christian life in the marketplace, most likely you are a pretender in the Church world. Paul withstood all the worldly temptations without compromising his testimony. He modeled business and marketplace ethics as well as morality in a way that should inspire all marketplace ministers.

> *"If you are a thief, quit stealing. Instead, use your hands for good hard work, and then give generously to others in need"* Ephesians 4:28 (NLT).

> *"Make it your goal to live a quiet life, minding your own business and working with your hands, just as we instructed you before. Then people who are not Christians will respect the way you live your life, and will not need to depend on you"* I Thessalonians 4:11-12

(NLT).

Paul had at least four primary motives for the way he lived and worked in the marketplace. First, in I Thessalonians 2 and 4 he makes clear his love to share the Gospel as he shared his life. Second, he serves as a model for all Christians as a worker and disciple in the marketplace. Third, he won the respect of those outside the "household of faith." Fourth, he modeled a strong "ambition" to live a quiet and orderly life, not withdrawn from society, but with integrity in a "dog-eat-dog" world.

There was no question in Paul's mind as to his marketplace mission. According to I Corinthians 1:16, Paul was committed to converting entire households. Being of Jewish heritage and Roman citizenship helped him develop a broad and wide social network. The marketplace provided a context for him to operate a profitable tent making business where he could offer the Gospel in real life and real time situations without restraint.

This is an opportunity that most five-fold gift ministers will never have the joy of experiencing on a regular basis. I have had far more opportunities to share the Gospel on the cutting edge of society, the streets and the marketplace, than I ever had inside the church facility.

Paul's strategy was reaching and influencing the major urban centers of his day. His work primarily centered around four major urban centers: Athens, Ephesus, Corinth and Rome. He felt that if he reached the major city of a region, the entire region was reached. He planted churches on the frontiers of the Gospel where Christ was not known according to Romans 15:20. He strengthened and matured churches he had already planted. He had a ministry to the Jews but was called to be an Apostle to the Gentiles. None of this would have happened the way it did without his call and passion for the marketplace.

Paul said the leaders of the Church had nothing to add to what he was preaching. Their reputation as great leaders made no difference to Paul for God has no favorites and he knew it. Instead, he said they saw God has given me the responsibility of preaching to the Gentiles just as He has given Peter the responsibility of preaching to the Jews—a most unlikely candidate I might add.

Paul felt the same God who had worked through Peter as the apostle to the Jews, also worked through him as the apostle to the Gentiles. In fact, James, Peter and John, known as pillars of the Church, recognized the gift God gave Paul and accepted Barnabas and Paul as their coworkers. They encouraged Paul and Barnabas to keep preaching to the Gentiles, while they continued their work with the Jews.

Why the marketplace and why now? Because it was the centerpiece of the first-century church and if the

Church fulfills its Matthew 28 mandate, it must be the centerpiece of every generation including today's. Presently, the Church is making some gains in evangelizing some areas of the world, especially Asia and Africa. Church planting organizations are active and making progress in reaching the unreached people groups in these regions. Nevertheless, efforts in the marketplace are minimal at best and idle in most of the world's "supermarkets" where most significant economic decisions are made.

Jesus and Paul had many reasons for going to the marketplace that went beyond their need for money. I am sure they knew that is where the need for the Gospel message was the greatest. That first-century church was anything but idle in the marketplace of their day. Signs and wonders were more common in the marketplace than in the house church meetings they attended.

In fact, of the 39 "power miracles" recorded in the book of Acts, 38 happened in the marketplace. The gift of evangelist was alive and well in the marketplace. That suggests the reason we have so many idle evangelists. They are trying to exercise their gift in the church house where it is easy; when their gift and anointing is for the marketplace if that is truly the gift God gave them. If you can't get results in the marketplace with your so-called gifting then the odds are good you don't have one.

Not Every Traveling Minister Is An Evangelist

We call everyone who travels from church to church an evangelist whether they have the gift or not. I believe it has caused confusion in the body of Christ and done a disservice to those who have the gift as well as to those who do not. A true evangelist is gifted to share the Gospel with those who have never heard and help all believers be comfortable sharing their faith with their own personality.

Paul told Timothy, "Do the work of an evangelist." Most who travel as evangelists are functionally revivalist, teachers, exhorters, "music-narians" and other valid ministers, but certainly not evangelists. The gift of evangelist is needed more in the marketplace than in the church world. I will go as far to say that evangelists who spend their time going from church to church are something other than true evangelists.

A friend of mine heard a story about an evangelist named Reinhard Bonnke. He was visiting a local church back in the 80's in order to raise support for his efforts in Africa. According to Reinhard, he couldn't keep his mind on the church service because all he could think about was the local disco-tech where most of the city's youth hung out on Saturday night. After service, he grabbed a few youth and made his way to the disco-tech with heart pounding.

He asked the manager if he could have the

microphone for five minutes claiming he came all the way from Africa to speak to the youth. Amazingly, the manager agreed and gave him the center floor for five minutes.

Reinhard gave a simple gospel message and then asked who wanted to know "this Jesus." Youth started weeping throughout the disco-tech. Many came to Christ that night. A year later, he returned to that same church for another meeting. One of the youth picked him up at the airport and told him he had a surprise for him. He took him past the former disco-tech on the way to his hotel.

What was once the seat of action for the youth of that city was now a church fulfilling God's commission in the world. He went inside and was surrounded by young people saying, "I was the one who used to work the lights!" and another said, "I was the one who worked the concessions! We are now serving Jesus!" That is an evangelist.

Paul chose to answer the call to the marketplace because it helped him model a lifestyle that other Christians could emulate easier than the lifestyle of a professional five-fold gift minister. He validated the genuine call to and ministry in the marketplace. Paul proved marketplace ministry is not a secondary or inferior call to that of the five-fold gift ministry, but a compliment.

His call to the marketplace put him in relationship

with a vast network of potential followers of Christ, but most of all, it helped him prove that the Christian life is not simply a religious belief system, but a way of life making you an overcomer in every area of life, including the marketplace.

When the Church begins to recognize and affirm the call to the marketplace with the same esteem as they do the five-fold gift ministry, you will begin to see more activity resembling Paul's ministry in the marketplace of his day. When activity at the church house is given priority over the marketplace, the marketplace remains idle.

When activity at the church is not relevant to the marketplace, there will be little motivation for most Christians to be active in either place or little motivation for marketplace people to come there.

As long as the Church does more to fill its house with warm bodies than it does to fill the marketplace with trained soldiers, the marketplace remains idle. As long as the Church spends most of its time and energy motivating members to respond to institutional concerns, it has little left to equip its members to be first responders in the marketplace.

Why the marketplace? Because that is where the real battles for the souls of men are fought and won or lost. Why now? Because every day approximately 156,000 people die while their eternal destiny hangs in the balance. How much longer can the Church afford to remain idle in the marketplace.

"And about the eleventh hour he went out, found others standing, and saith unto them, Why stand ye here all the day idle?" Matthew 20:6 (ASV)

ABOUT THE AUTHOR

Since 1966, Dr. Robinson has developed his leadership and management skills through a wide range of opportunities in both the church world and the marketplace. For 39 years, he served in pastoral ministry as Senior Pastor or Associate Pastor for churches in Pennsylvania, Massachusetts, and Illinois. Along with his wife Marie and family, he has lived and ministered in the Chicago area since 1979.

He has a Bachelor of Applied Theology from Logos Christian College, Master of *Organizational Leadership* from Southern Seminary and a PhD from Aidan University. In the marketplace, he has held various leadership positions in the retail and wholesale industry.

From 2002-05 he owned a successful multi-million dollar Recreational Vehicle Dealership in Chicago.

Since 2005, he has served as a full-time ministry coach for leaders in the Church, Marketplace, Government and Education. He travels 200+ days a year helping leaders improve their leadership skills and see their vision become a reality.

16551525R00121

Made in the USA
Charleston, SC
27 December 2012